Resolving Grief

*Strategies for Coping with Loss
through Faith*

Jim Towns, Ph.D.

Resolving Grief
by Jim Towns

Printed in the United States of America

ISBN 1-594674-33-7

Unless otherwise noted, Scripture quotations are taken from The New King James Version / Thomas Nelson Publishers, Nashville: Thomas Nelson Publishers., Copyright © 1982. Used by permission. All rights reserved.

Scripture quotations marked "NLT" are taken from the HOLY BIBLE, New Living Translation copyright © 1996 by Tyndale Charitable Trust. Used by permission of Tyndale House Publishers.

Produced with the assistance of Fluency in Tyler, Texas.

www.xulonpress.com

This book is presented to:

_____

*With the sincere hope that
working together can
help in the healing
process of
resolving grief*

From:

_____

Table of Contents

Acknowledgments

Regardless of what the title page may assert, no one ever writes a book alone. In observance of this assertion, I must declare my indebtedness to those individuals with whom I have come in contact and whose ideas may have slipped unconsciously into my perspective—perhaps to have surfaced here as my own. For such contributions of content and encouragement, neither syllable nor sentence grants me an adequate means for expression of my gratitude. I must simply defer to both humble reverence and acknowledgement.

Despite the beloved assistance I received while completing this work, this book does not provide easy answers to the complex questions surrounding loss and grief. Rather, it boldly addresses the hardships often elicited in such instances and assures us that the sometimes seemingly erratic and "abnormal" spectrum of emotions we experience (or perhaps lack thereof) is normal and indeed necessary for our return to a satisfying existence in the wake of personal loss. I have taken the "best of the best" from my previous published works and inserted significant additions to provide even more clarity and insight on this most important topic of resolving grief.

*This book is presented
in gratitude to God for His love and grace,
in appreciation to my family and friends for their
understanding,
and in memory of a lovely lady who
lived for others and paid the price for my
knowledge concerning grief:
Mona Hancock Towns*

Introduction

Few other events are as life changing as the death of someone one deeply loves! As I have been deeply acquainted with death, loss, and grief, I found it necessary to write this book. In a short span of time, I lost several family members and friends. If there would have been an award given for the world's most inept griever, I would have certainly and easily won the contest. As many often do, I treated my thoughts and feelings (all normal grief behavior) as if they were abnormal. Although I was unaware at the time, my self-imposed irrationality only served to prolong my anguish and defy any sense of inner peace.

I soon learned, however, it is *normal* to experience disturbing emotions throughout the grieving process...a discovery that became the main thrust of my desire to help others in bereavement. As an extension of that mission, I also wanted to be able to present individuals and families in fresh sorrow with a brief, practical tool to help them understand the rigors and patterns in the sequence of normal grief behavior.

The tools offered in this book, forged in the fires of experience, have proven to be effective. I don't consider this book a complex theological or philosophical work, only a simple, direct statement of what behavior is like when a person is in bereavement. Perhaps we have been too cautious in overprotecting others from thinking about death in a deeply personal way. Therefore, without reservation, I hope to reveal what I regard as some of the most profound and useful insights for assisting in the acceptance of death's inevitability and purpose rather than shielding ourselves from it.

People in search of answers to grief have looked to philosophy, psychology, sociology, science, and religion. The *theologian* wants to know what God has said about life, death and the afterlife. The *biologist* tries to define death and determine when it actually occurs. The *psychologist* is concerned with how people face their own death as well as their reactions to the deaths of significant others. The *sociologist* investigates how value systems, lifestyles, and attitudes of societies cause people to deal with loss and grief. Meanwhile, the *philosopher*, *poet*, and *artist* try to describe the experience of a life ending. Please do not misunderstand; all such manner of inquisition is good, if used appropriately.

However, if I am honest, I must use my intellectual integrity and give faith an opportunity to work in my life and afford an explanation of certain mysterious events. In writing this book, I imagined readers who personify the spiritual perspective of Mark 9:24, "I believe, help my unbelief." Therefore, I designed *Resolving Grief* to try to explain the logic of faith while contemplating the perplexing issues of life and death. We have a better chance of dealing realistically with death if we realize in advance that it could happen to us at any time.

I realize that many times when a tragedy occurs, people harshly tend to blame God for what has happened. This book presents the scriptural perspective of the human being as a free moral agent interacting with the mystery of God's natural law and sovereignty. Thus, it is a practical statement about how to respond effectively within the process of normal grief while adhering to our declarations of faith. Despite the firmness with which I make the above statements, readers are free to accept or reject such a supposition. Regardless, my basic hope is that people will learn to treat their normal grief behavior as such and refrain from its defiance.

One final word. Please note that I intentionally did not title this book, "Solving Grief." While there are no easy solutions, there are resolutions. *Resolving Grief* is about adjustment while resolving grief. It is for those who are grieving and for those who desire to understand sorrow so that they may afford others comfort and understanding. If these ideas stimulate questions, discussion, and provide some answers, they will have served a meaningful purpose.

If we will think, plan, and prepare to accept grief and sorrow as a part of life, perhaps we will avoid the dangerous trend of treating our normal grief behavior as something to be avoided and suppressed.

Jim Towns, Ph.D.
Department of Communication
Stephen F. Austin State University
Nacogdoches, TX 75962-6174
jtowns@sfasu.edu

Grief is not an option, but recovery is!

Part One:
Why Did This Happen?

Death is one of the most predominant fears known to humankind. In fact, the theologian and philosopher, Paul Tillich, pointed out that most people harbor some level of conscious anxiety regarding the issue of life's termination. Thoughts as to the manner and time of our death flood our minds on occasion.

The uneasiness with which this inner dialogue often occurs may be due in part to the frightening fact that death may occur at any time. For while we are painfully aware that death is inevitable, there seldom seems to be an opportune time for any of us to die. In this section, we'll study the natural response people have when they lose someone they love or suddenly face the reality of their own impending death.

CHAPTER ONE

Why Did This Happen?

resolving (ri-zolv-ing), *adj.* in the process of solving.

grief (gref), *n.* deep sadness, heavy sorrow resulting from loss.

If I could sit down with God face to face, I would reiterate the famous question of the British author and theologian, C. S. Lewis, who said, "Why did 'this' have to happen?" Immediately following God's answer to my inquiry, I would still probably ask, "But why?" If this perspective sounds familiar, then I hope the following ideas will present some resolve to the question of "Why?"

Despite its existence as a global link, the subject of death remains a taboo topic for many. Its morbid stigma often proves too unsettling for discussion and thus falls prey to avoidance. In spite of such silence, death continues to fuel individual concern as well as a desire for most people to know more about the available coping mechanisms that can ease their personal grief.

It is helpful to look at every death as a touching love story—a unique and special drama, just as we might consider each birth. Both birth and death occupy significant roles and are shrouded in deep meaning. Thus, we should avoid neither but embrace them, for it is during such moments that we experience the true essence of life.

We Want to Know Why

Consider grief. If you have known it, you will remember its icy grip. If you have not yet lost someone you love, then imagine yourself suddenly thrust into an alien world. Your body is weary; your emotions are raw. Your heartache is transformed from a mere cliché into a source of true physical pain. You are convinced that your life as you once knew it has ceased to exist. You do not know how to think, how to stop feeling, how to start feeling, what to do, and what not to do. Knowledge cannot erase our emotions that accompany sorrow, but knowledge can help guide us toward resolution and recovery.

The fact that contemporary society allocates little time for death only serves to compound the complications death elicits. We typically handle a death quickly, and many just as rapidly forget it. Yet grief remains and so does our greatest task emerging from the resulting sorrow. We must accept changes in family unity while mustering the ability to function in our everyday lives in a manner that does not allow grief to destroy us or those closest to us. The degree of success to which we are able to achieve such a feat often determines the expediency with which we are able to move forward and regain optimum quality of life.

Choosing to Learn

In light of our discussion thus far, it has become apparent that death is not an elective, but learning about death is! Television affords such a choice as it continues to project explicit images of death into our living rooms. Yet despite death's prominence in much of today's programming, we are still shocked when mortality's thievery invades our own reality.

Saturation with death through mass media does not prepare us for dealing with it, but perhaps it conversely conditions us to believe that death happens only to "other" people. The ramifications of such a profoundly false theory leave us reeling in disbelief and searching desperately for answers.

Though death is a fact of life, many try to deny it. One of my friends described death as "an ever-present boundary to life, which causes us to find meaning in life; yet if we constantly dwell upon death, life will never be lived!" Thus, the reality of death is not merely a possibility articulated with such phrases as, "If something happens to us…," but it is rather a confirmation stated as, "*When* something happens to us…"

However, even though dying is as much a part of life and development as being born, this truth does not have to be the bearer of depression and sorrow. We can choose to learn to accept it as a culmination of our life experience. As the writer of Ecclesiastes profoundly stated, "There is a time for everything…a time to be born and a time to die" (Ecclesiastes 3:1–2).

When the death of a loved one occurs, most people experience a period when they question the validity and purpose of their own existence. In order to better endure such a lofty mission, we must employ both reason and faith. Some people feel that it is rude or presumptuous to question such instances over which we can exert little or no control. However, it depends on whether the question is an honest search in faith for meaning or whether it is a challenge of disbelief or rebellion.

Answer or Argument?

The erroneous pursuit of "Why?" usually does not call for an answer as much as it calls for an argument. We demand to know the definitive "Why?" while in our grief. We want concrete answers and immediate comfort. We desire to know the "Why?" as opposed to resolving the mystery.

Ultimately, however, I have come to realize there is a grand scheme of design of which I have little logistical knowledge. God alone is sovereign in the design of life and death. The "Why?" of an honest search for answers is not the same as the rebellious, belligerent "Why?" type of questioning. The right kind of questioning can bring about much desired comfort and relief while the wrong form of this mission often brings forth more inconsistencies, often resulting in anger and dismay.

My first experience with death in my immediate

family resulted in an agonizingly slow resolve to a new normal life. Had I been aware of the normal grief process, I would have still mourned, of course, but this knowledge would have afforded me a blueprint of sorts for finding some comfort. Perhaps I would have better known how to analyze my bewildering emotions and erratic behavior. I had so many unanswered questions and feelings. I believe such information would have granted me a more expedient recovery.

It is normal to ask why this has happened to us, but if we are to find answers, we must seek out those resources that will ultimately provide them. It is my intention that the following insights will prove to be helpful along your journey to discover these resources.

CHAPTER TWO

Resolving the "Why" Questions

Although there are often no satisfying answers to solve the primary question of why death occurs, there are indeed secondary principles that emerge from an appropriate quest for truth. These principles prove helpful in resolving the "why" and/or "how" things happen. There are four such principles, and they include laws of nature, human imperfection, community living, and divine impartiality. Understanding these principles can provide clues as to what created the possibility for the loss to happen and perhaps bring about some comfort.

Principle One: Laws of Nature

In my own experience with loss, I first turned to logic to provide answers as to why the death in my family had occurred. I was aware of the inevitability of death and thought that if I could attain logical reasons and/or purposes for the event, I could better accept my losses.

This line of thinking yielded the initial idea that suffering and tragedy are caused neither by gross and terrible sins that we have committed nor simply by the judgmental will of God. We must realize that God does not randomly and impersonally will tragedy upon us. If we trust Him, He is the God of love who is there to take care of us in all aspects of life and death. However, we often find an odd sense of comfort in placing blame on God for something we possibly could have brought on ourselves or might have resulted from random events we were powerless to prevent.

Why is there suffering and sorrow in the world? Scripture teaches us that many times the sorrow and suffering in the world are the direct and indirect result of sin. Sin is simply the breaking of God's law or that which interferes with our having an adequate relationship with God. Consequently, as dictated by biblical instruction, such action warrants death. As God said to Adam and Eve, "In the day that you eat of it you shall surely die," (Genesis 2:17). Paul also provided insight on the penalty of sin, "The wages of sin is death," (Romans 6:23).

The physical death described above is the transition or separation of body and spirit. Such a death results in the decay of the body (Ecclesiastes 12:7) and is part of the penalty of sin. If there had been no commission of sin, there would have been no physical death. In other words, Adam and Eve would not have died had they not sinned. Yet this event ushered death into our world and has continued to prevail for every living human being.

The laws of nature, death being one of them, are indiscriminant. God set natural law into motion with the creation of physical life. The natural world has both assets—beauty, wealth, and the like—as well as liabilities including disease, tornadoes, floods, and earthquakes.

As one of the liabilities mentioned above, disease is often shrouded in mystery. There are often no simple answers for why some people contract diseases while others appear to never grow ill. God does not make people get sick; nor does He indiscriminately will disease upon a person. If, in fact, we do blame God for such misfortune, we may do so from an inadequate theological base or incorrect concept of who He is and how He works. Although many may become satisfied to blame God for their loss and halt their inquiry, I implore you not to tarry too long in such thought. Instead, intensify your search for answers. For despite the randomness that may not appear indicative of a merciful God, we must remember there is often mystery in the ways of God!

Let's examine the concept of natural law a bit further. The material environment of our world maintains its stability in the fact that it is law-abiding. The rain may aid one set of human purposes (to relieve a drought and grow crops) and harm another (to flood a vulnerable coastal village). It may seem at times that the world and environment are cruel and hopeless, but there is stability in the mere fact that life on this earth continues to regenerate despite its perpetual loss.

For instance, God does not always heal the diseased physical body. A Christian doctor once related that he prays for healing—if it is God's will. He never tells patients that they will be physically healed if they "have enough faith." People who assert such a statement are often strangely inconsistent as they themselves may wear false teeth, glasses, and other artificial aids! If faith were the primary determinant of our ability to heal and/or be free of ailment, wouldn't these individuals be void of impairments requiring such manufactured assistance?

In the Bible, this principle could be deemed the "economy of the miraculous." In other words, God does not always work a miracle when a normal channel is available, and He does not always intervene when the case at hand is medically hopeless. Quite simply, losses can happen due to the laws of nature of which perhaps we are unaware or blatantly choose to ignore. The latter explanation brings us to the next consideration, human imperfection.

Principle Two: Human Imperfection

Humans have a frail framework. They cannot always see what is best or right in ultimate terms. People make decisions and must live with the consequences, whether good or bad. As stated earlier, many times people blame God for accidents or mistakes that actually result from our own decisions. The real reasons for such dire circumstances are often due to human imperfection.

For example, consider a plane that crashes

during a storm as a demonstration of such human imperfection in the decision-making process. Aware of the turbulent conditions, the pilot and crew have several options of recourse. They can go around the storm, increase their altitude and fly over it, or they can simply turn back. Yet, in our example, they decide that they can withstand the elements and forge ahead. Unfortunately, the raging storm proves worse than they anticipated, and all aboard perish. Quite obviously, the tragic plane crash came because of human imperfection: the flight crew's failure to choose the most reasonable course of action that would have ensured their safety as well as that of the passengers. Similarly, if drivers would act more responsibly and be considerate of one another, many automobile accidents could be avoided. Unfortunately, if automobiles can go fast enough to provide needed transportation, they can also go fast enough to destroy lives.

Disease may also result from imperfect reasoning. We reason that food is delicious as we gorge ourselves relentlessly. Perhaps elements in our diets react against the physical body, allowing diseases to find their beginnings. In fact, most processed food products are not healthful, yet our sensory needs to taste and enjoy these foods outweigh the foreboding costs.

Yet another example of human error may lie in the fact that we do not do the right thing at the right time in order to avoid or prevent illness. We may not seek medical attention at the proper time by failing to grant our symptoms the immediacy they deserve. Thus, we reap the consequences of our waning powers of reason.

However, despite our responsibility in such matters, many times we ask why God does not "do something" to help us! Meanwhile, He is probably wondering why we do not utilize the gift of knowledge and ability He gave us and thus prevent harm or injury.

While some losses do indeed happen due to individual human imperfection as illustrated above, we must remember we live within communities of imperfect people. Tragedies may happen because of the misfortunate decisions and choices of others.

Principle Three: Community Living

Although we profess the self-protective axiom of our culture, "Looking out for number one," our proximity in an overcrowded world negates the possibility of isolation. There is no such thing as

"Me, myself and I" in the modern world. As population figures explode, so does the realization that what one person does often has an effect on others. For example, when one person gets the flu, usually many more develop similar symptoms. Such physical epidemics take their toll, as do the circumstances exerted on others from our own actions.

When I was in college, a young man climbed to the top of the tower on the University of Texas campus in Austin. He pulled out a gun and began shooting students in all directions. Ultimately, in the wake of numerous fatalities, the man shot himself. Because he lived in a populated community, the gunman, Charles Whitman, not only hurt himself while on that now infamous tower; he also harmed 21 other people. If Whitman had been on a deserted island, his irrational behavior would not have exerted such a profound impact. However, because he acted within community, his actions brought about irreversible consequences for numerous innocent people.

Although blatantly senseless, we have only to open the morning paper to see the evidence of such erratic actions bringing harm or death to innocent multitudes across our nation and world. In community living, tragedies may also result if people are not responsible and fail to be considerate of one another. For example, alcohol and substance abuse have taken an overwhelming toll on the masses. Each year, numerous individuals have been harmed or killed by others acting under the influence of alcohol or other mind-altering drugs.

However, perhaps the most powerful illustration encompassing all three principles we've studied thus far (laws of nature, human imperfection and community living) is the historic "Attack on America" which occurred on September 11, 2001. Unprecedented in its scope of casualties, this domestic attack brought about global awareness regarding the vulnerability we exhibit at all times. Furthermore, when examined more closely, this event also clearly demonstrates numerous elements of our next point of discussion—divine impartiality.

Principle Four: Divine Impartiality

"Good" and "bad" happen to everyone. Events and situations we typically consider "good" are imparted to both good and bad individuals. The allocation of "bad" also follows this confusing pattern. Thus, these polarized opposites sporadically shower the just and unjust.

Think about the New Testament parable of the

two houses that stood on opposing foundations of sand and rock (Matthew 7:24–27). Identical storms, rain, and wind assailed both structures. They did not just afflict the obviously weaker house built upon a sandy base. While the house on the rock did indeed remain steadfast, it too endured the ravages of the unsavory elements. Same storm, different result. Similarly, if the foundation of a person's life is God's Word, he or she may not be exempt from life's storms but will assuredly remain standing during and after the troubling experiences endured throughout a lifetime.

When I was in deep sorrow, going through just such a "storm," doubts flooded my mind. At a major crisis point, I made the following statement of commitment in my personal journal:

"As I walk the way of loss that has produced doubt, uncertainty, and rank skepticism, I'm not afraid to entrust an unknown immediate future to my known God.

So many things have happened that could make my actions be based on superstition instead of spiritual direction. At times, I've prayed for healing and it "worked" from my perspective. Yet, at other times, the same prayer yielded nothing as far as I was concerned.

I've endeavored in many such seemingly worthwhile activities that have produced inconsistent results. Even so, I'm not afraid to entrust an unknown immediate future to my known God.

When I question why, I realize that God wants me to know. He says to me, 'My little child, if you could see it the way I see it, you would not worry. You would know that I am taking care of you in a very special way.'

I'm not afraid to entrust an unknown immediate future to my known God."

Later on, I became aware that the grumbling I had sustained in response to my various situations and unanswered questions was not in opposition of what I viewed as dire circumstances; they were against God Himself! I didn't just resent the circumstances. I resented God for allowing me, of all people, to be in the circumstances. Gratefully, I believe Scripture teaches it is God's nature to remain faithful to me even during such times, as He does with all humans, despite the fact that we insist on trusting ourselves, friends, family, and society rather than our Creator.

In order to understand divine impartiality and adjust, we must try to think more clearly from God's perspective. How do we accomplish that?

We learn how He thinks through His Word. We must respond, "Thank you, Lord. You are in charge" (see 1 Thessalonians 5:18).

We must also remember that God is sovereign. The Bible teaches that the devil, our adversary, cannot afflict people until God permits him to do so. In the Book of Job, we have the story of a righteous, God-fearing man who lost his possessions, his loved ones, and his health—all in a single day. Job asked why all the sorrow and grief had befallen him. After all, he was a good man. He questioned God's methodology and countered that he alone in his human wisdom knew of a more effective path. In response, God asked Job probing questions that soundly proved God's providence and sovereignty (chapters 38–41). "Where were you when I laid the foundations of the earth? Tell me, if you know so much. Do you know how its dimensions were determined and who did the surveying?" (Job 38:4–5, NLT).

When Job realized who God was and the enormity of His heavenly perspective, he responded to God, "I am nothing—how could I ever find the answers? I will put my hand over my mouth in silence. I have said too much already. I have nothing more to say" (Job 40:4–5 NLT). The poignancy of this story is that God never granted Job a definitive answer as to why the losses occurred in his life. So, too, this story reminds us that we can only *resolve* our grief, not *solve* it.

God's Past Faithfulness, Future Intervention

Throughout my search, some of the answers to my whys have been revealed in the fact that God dared to show me what a sinful man I am and what still remains in my subconscious. God did not trust me so much as He trusted Himself in me (meaning, the presence of Christ within me through the indwelling Holy Spirit). Therefore, He permitted the darkness of the storm to approach and continued to work (although often seemingly absent) amid the darkness of the situation at hand.

The following statement is perhaps one of the most meaningful spiritual insights God has granted me. I penned these words at a crucial point in my life, *"Perceive today in the light of God's past faithfulness and future intervention."* The God who has been faithful to us in our past will also be faithful in future intervention.

If we will take the time to reflect, we all have specific illustrations of how God has met our needs in the past. Therefore, the seeds of potential faith to depend on His future interventions are in these past experiences.

While trying to discover primarily why things had to happen the way they did, there finally comes a time when we, like Job, back off and admit, "I do not know." We walk in the light we have been given and perceive today in the light of God's past faithfulness and future intervention. We live our lives forward, but most of the time we *understand* in retrospect! Nineteenth century evangelist Charles Spurgeon gives us more insight, "God is too good to be unkind, too wise to be mistaken. When we cannot trace His hand, we must always trust His heart." Rather than ask for answers to unanswerable questions, I can thank God for the life and work of the loved one who is now deceased.

Questions to Consider

The following questions are provided for individual reflection and/or group discussion. You may wish to work through these questions all at once or perhaps one at a time. Above all, consider them at your own pace. You might wish to journal your reflections on these questions as part of a meditation time or talk about them with a trusted family member or friend in quiet conversation. Some might use the material as part of a recovery group format. However you choose to use this feature of the book, spend time reflecting on each question as it relates to your recovery process.

1. Why is our pursuit of definitive answers to the "why" questions concerning loss so harmful?

2. What is a positive, appropriate pursuit of trying to discover answers to the "why" concerning loss? Give examples.

3. How do you see "Principle One: Laws of Nature" affecting your loss?

4. How does "Principle Two: Human Imperfection" relate to how your loss happened?

5. Give examples of how "Principle Three: Community Living" can help someone understand loss.

6. What parts of "Principle Four: Divine Impartiality" are the most difficult for you to understand? Why?

7. What does it mean to "Perceive today in the light of God's past faithfulness and future intervention"?

8. What will you do as result of understanding the ideas that helped you the most?

Part Two:
The Normal Grief Process

Grief is often a double-edged sword. On one side, there is relief because someone is out of difficulty and pain; on the other side, there is grief because we will miss him or her. As there are infinite variations of emotional response to loss, human grief defies abbreviated explanation. Can we make any sense out of the conflicting emotions? In this section, I will provide a sequential process that bridges the gap between the spiritual and humanistic philosophies concerning grief. Think of this model as signposts for those individuals wandering grief's frosty path to identify where they are and where they are likely going in the process.

Such a dissection of bereavement is vital because maladjustment to grief results when people fail to understand the "normal" grieving process. In other words, they get "lost" in the dark shadow of grief. Perhaps of even greater significance is the way one perceives the grief. In other words, it is not so much what happened as it is how you felt concerning the loss/grief. Perhaps grieving individuals have never been confronted with the issue; or, quite simply, self-preservation has negated the thought of preparing for our undeniable end of life on earth or that of our loved ones.

Such novice tendencies lead many who encounter personal loss to treat their "normal" behavior as if it were something to be avoided and thus deny themselves the necessary pathway to recovery. Only education and illumination of grief's characteristics can afford anyone comfort in death's wake.

CHAPTER THREE

When Crises Occur

No matter how brave and strong we are, or perhaps think we are, we must call grief or sorrow by its appropriate name in order to comprehend its magnitude. In one sense, grief is the feeling of a bruised soul from a significant loss. We should not minimize what we are going through by any reflection or twist of words when death removes a member of our family or a friend. Rather, we should embrace one very important fact—someone we love is deceased; he or she is no longer with us. We are human, and we will indeed grieve the individual's departure and absence from our daily lives.

Despite its spiritual or secular base, this grief to which we continue to allude is the process through which we readjust to our environment and create new life despite the absence of the deceased. More succinctly stated, *"Grief is a series of thoughts, feelings, and actions during a period of adjustment to the loss of a loved one."* Denial of this process can only serve to our detriment and halt our ability to function normally once again. Therefore, familiarizing ourselves with such a progression of emotion is imperative to those of us whose wish to recapture the quality of our previous existence.

Stages of Grief

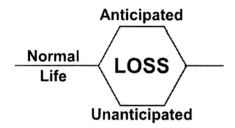

TOWNS DIAGRAM© OF
NORMAL GRIEF PROCESS
Graphic 1

In order to understand the diagram of normal grief, let's think in terms of the journey of life. In this analogy, we are journeying along on the highway of a comfortable, normal life. Suddenly, whether anticipated or unanticipated, a loss happens (see Graphic 1).

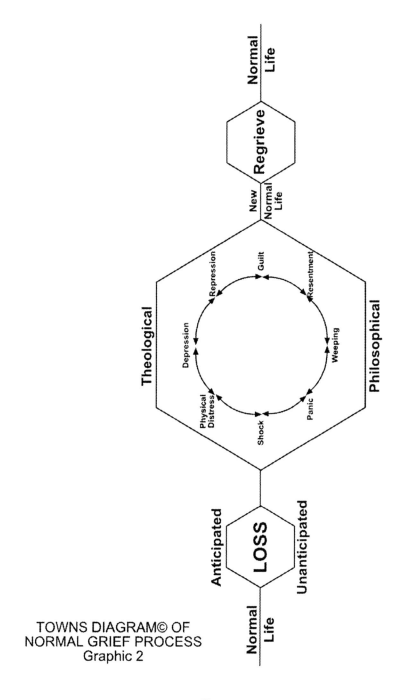

TOWNS DIAGRAM© OF
NORMAL GRIEF PROCESS
Graphic 2

As we encounter the loss, we reevaluate our philosophical as well as theological perspectives of life cycling through the components of normal grief (see Graphic 2). After all, this is no longer normal life as we knew it. After processing the components for a while, we grow weary of being "sick and tired" and stricken with grief. We then realize that life does go on and thus choose to keep on living. At this point, we may be granted resolve toward a new normal life despite the absence of what we have lost.

However, as we can see in our model, there will be times on the journey when we once again regrieve our loss. These regrieving times will likely be significant calendar dates such as Christmas, anniversaries, birthdays, etc. Yet we can continue to regain a normal life once more.

Each individual does not necessarily go through all the stages of grief; nor does he or she go through them in the same manner or order presented here. However, despite the degree of intensity or sequence of the actual experience, the normal grief process has often been found to include the following: Shock, Weeping, Panic, Resentment, Guilt, Repression, Depression, and Physical Distress. Denial weaves itself throughout the components and process. Although this list is not all encompassing of the emotional spectrum one encounters, it does serve as a base for our discussion and one from which we can glean understanding.

Shock – Denial

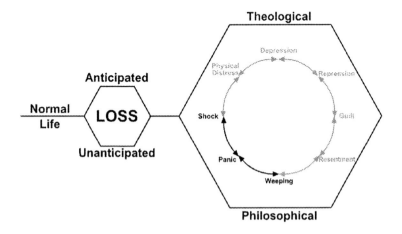

TOWNS DIAGRAM© OF
NORMAL GRIEF PROCESS
Graphic 3

Shock is a blow, impact, or sudden agitation of the mental or emotional sensibilities (see Graphic 3). We may experience a numbing reaction immediately upon hearing about the death of someone we love. It may last only a few minutes or perhaps several hours or days. On many occasions, when I have learned of the death of someone dear to me, I have been stunned. I have walked around in the proverbial trance or daze we often associate with feelings of disbelief. I could hear people talking to me, but the words or sounds did not register fully. I was quite simply numb to my normal sensory perception.

Despite this obvious suspension of normalcy, do not be afraid of this initial shock. It is to be expected and may actually serve as the body's physical defense to the sometimes seemingly unbearable grip of grief. However, if the duration of shock and denial becomes extensive, perhaps lasting several weeks, the situation can become grave or even unhealthy. Such instances may require professional assistance or heightened interaction with loved ones. Thus, it is obvious that making a distinction between short episodes of shock and those of a lingering nature should be immediate.

Perhaps the best method of treatment for those experiencing shock is to keep him or her fairly busy by carrying on as much usual activity as possible throughout the time of crisis. The sooner the individual has to deal with immediate problems and subsequent decision-making, the better. If such activity does not ensue quickly, he or she could forego a great deal of self-confidence and possibly lose touch with reality. Thus, we should be easily accessible for assistance yet not hinder the therapeutic value of allowing these individuals to "do for themselves."

In addition to the emotional shock indicated above, social shock may also accompany a loss. For example, a married person upon losing a spouse is suddenly single again. They are thrust into the social shock of existing and functioning in society from an isolated state rather than from the comfortable familiarity of a partnership. This scenario may be compounded by the fact that well-meaning relatives and friends may understandably fumble as well in their adjustment to the situation. Thus, once again, support from those closest to the individual becomes imperative as shock, either emotional, social or both, may result in the next stage of the grief process—panic.

Panic

Panic is sudden, severe, overpowering fright (see Graphic 3). Such emotion often emerges when we become consumed by our grief and seem powerless to entertain any thoughts other than those related to our loss. The past, present, and future converge and overtake our consciousness, thus overriding our coping capabilities. I have experienced such helplessness, as my mind was only capable of a few seconds of freedom from the memory of my loss and the grief that it entailed. While the experience was truly frightening, this inability to concentrate is indeed normal and natural during the grieving process.

Panic may also arise out of a fear of the unknown or things we do not understand. Therefore, it's important to seek an understanding of the grief process prior to undergoing it! This information can help negate such instances of panic or, if panic does arise, it will keep one from considering it abnormal.

The first time I experienced deep sorrow, I did not know what to expect. I thought my life had derailed from any sense of normalcy and was perhaps doomed to an unsavory alteration from which I may be unable to surface. In short, I began to panic. I even felt that I was losing my mind because of my inability to control my feelings, thoughts, or verbalizations. Perpetual gloom had become my companion, and I feared that I might relent to its power.

I was unaware that these instances were an integral part of my recovery process. Had I been more prepared, I may have averted such irrationality on my part.

Weeping

We cannot separate our emotions or weeping from the situations or experiences that evoke them (see Graphic 3). Tears are the overflow of pain inside the soul. Thus, when a person is experiencing grief from loss, weeping is the impulse evoked from the inner anguish he or she feels. Our emotions often arrive rather vehemently when we realize the full impact of what we have lost. These feelings may well up with an uncontrollable force that our bodies are unable to contain. The pressure becomes too great and is unleashed in an expression of grief. The first step in dealing with such weeping is to recognize it as a normal occurrence and realize that it is actually working to relieve inner pressure and stress. Therefore, we should simply allow ourselves to weep and purge the emotions that we continue to encounter.

While weeping may appear as a common ritual for most, some people remain reluctant. For example, in American society, it is difficult for some men to cry openly. Perhaps this stems from being taught from a very early age that it is inappropriate for boys to cry due to a gender-imposed strength they are expected to uphold. As a result, many men feel that weeping is a sign of weakness and work to halt any such emotional displays.

However, we must realize that emotion (regard-less of gender) is an inside thermometer that rises and falls as a result of external events. To deny such release when needed can often cause people vari-ous problems—ones that may prove harder to over-come than any potential embarrassment they may have endured if they had simply extended their body its normal weeping outlet.

I have deemed a similar phenomenon "spiritual robotism" where one stifles any expression of sorrow upon hearing of the death of a loved one as a demonstration of great faith. Sometimes, people are simply embarrassed to show sorrow or weep openly. Although individuals are entitled to their own manner of dealing with loss, we should encourage the expression of grief. If such a display proves too difficult for some to reveal while surrounded by others, perhaps allow them stints of solitude so that their sorrow may take its natural course more privately.

Despite the amount of discussion allotted to the physical shedding of tears, we must realize weep-ing is only one of the ways to release our emotions. Perhaps we can express them to ourselves in writ-ing, articulate them to a friend, or even relay them to someone in a professional capacity. Whatever manner of emotional disposal we choose, it's important not to allow such feelings to remain bottled up inside of us.

There is truth in the idea that a joy shared doubles it and a sorrow shared halves it. Yet such expression may not prove to be a once-and-for-all event as implied. It is quite normal to weep intermittently for days, weeks or perhaps several months or years following the actual event. As mentioned, there are certain days in particular, however, that may prove most conducive to the shedding of tears. I call my tears on such occasions "love drops" as they are liquid love flowing from my eyes revealing a deep sense of emotion that I continue to feel for the departed. When weeping finally begins to subside, feelings of anger or resentment may soon take their place.

CHAPTER FOUR

Grief as a Process

We continue studying the normal grief process, resuming our place in the model—resentment or anger. Remember, individuals may experience these stages in random order and for varying lengths of time at each stage. However, for the sake of discussion, this model presents the typical process a person must go through in order to process grief appropriately.

Resentment-Anger

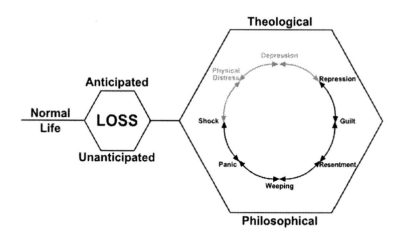

TOWNS DIAGRAM© OF
NORMAL GRIEF PROCESS
Graphic 4

Resentment and/or anger is the feeling of indignant displeasure because of something regarded as wrong (see Graphic 4). In other words, resentment is anger gone underground. In our grief, strong feelings of hostility and resentment may arise as we angrily, stubbornly try to make "things" the way they used to be. In fact, many who are in the grief process go through a period of being very critical of everything and everyone related to the loss. As individuals try to understand why the death occurred, they commence to blame others, expressing resentment to anyone who cared for their loved one. No matter what was done on behalf of the deceased, they feel that it was insufficient.

This type of resentment gives rise to such questions as, "Why did this happen?" and, "What could I have done to prevent it?" Remember, there are laws of nature, human imperfection, community living, and divine impartiality as we have discussed. Not all events have definitive causes or actions to blame. Despite this reality, many become so desperate in their resentment that they cannot live with themselves, much less with anyone else. Continuing in this volatile state only serves to hurt oneself more than anyone else one may feel is more deserving of pain.

It is comforting to note, however, that such behavior is often a common reality for those undergoing grief. It is also an identifiable precursor to feelings of guilt that may soon emerge.

Guilt

We often refer to normal guilt as the feeling of having committed a breach of conduct or the emotion one experiences when a person feels he or she has fallen short of expectations, either self-imposed or perhaps those imposed by others (see

Graphic 4). Yet another form of guilt can be neurotic or "false guilt" when it exists out of proportion to the individual's real involvement in a particular dilemma. In the context of personal loss, guilt often emerges as the latter type of feelings. For example, we believe that we should have been there to do or perhaps suggest something that may have been some comfort or assistance to the deceased prior to his or her death.

These negative guilt feelings may also come when we realize that we did not always treat the deceased in an appropriate manner. However, despite the understandable basis for our feelings, these often-misunderstood emotions can make us rather miserable for extended periods.

A good prescription for such guilt is in 1 John 1:9, "If we confess our sins, God is faithful and just to forgive us our sins and cleanse us from all unrighteousness." This verse implores us not to be afraid to talk about our feelings of guilt with those who care for us because airing these emotions can often expedite our healing. However, if such a reprieve from our guilt proves evasive and we are unable to make the situation or conditions better, repression may occur.

Repression

Repression is a defense behavior by which an individual prevents painful thoughts and desires from entering his or her conscious mind (see Graphic 4). We think of repression as occurring through omission. The thoughts are not truly forgotten; they simply keep coming back to the conscious mind in irregular intervals during which we may continue to send them back once again into the mental abyss.

Yet despite their apparent absence, these repressed feelings may continue to influence our behavior for extended periods. A person may be unaware of the real basis for a portion of his or her thoughts, beliefs, and actions. Eventually, however, he or she may discover that certain repressed emotions exist as the primary behind-the-scenes instigator of their various behavioral responses. For instance, if someone is trying to repress his or her feelings about the death of a loved one, and suddenly hears a favorite song shared with the deceased, he or she may break into tears. The person simply could not continue to repress the painful feelings bottled up inside.

Repressed feelings or thoughts may also become very active within the context of our dreams. Such manifestations may take various forms—some perhaps frightening—with others merely appearing as puzzling. When the person maintains these continued frustration levels that elicit such activity, an even more invasive situation may occur as the repressed thoughts may increase in strength and threaten to break through into the conscious mind and even into overt actions.

For instance, threats of mentally painful experiences lead to the arousal of anxiety and additional "fight or flight" defenses within the body. Repression may also diminish considerable mental energy needed to resolve the problems of those whose lives remain following a loss. All the activity going on behind-the-scenes in a person's mind and emotions lowers his or her defenses, decreasing morale and normal disposition. As a result, this negative energy enhances the individual's already compromised state.

Many times, when we allow repressed feelings to come into the conscious mind, resentment may arise because we have permitted the bruised emotions to be deeply felt again. We regress to resenting the loss itself and resenting the accompanying feelings. If repression is not adequately treated, then depression may emerge.

CHAPTER FIVE

Leading to Hope

In the height of the last stages of our model, depression and physical distress, it may be hard to believe that hope is around the corner. However, these last steps often lead to the eventual discovery that we are "sick and tired of being sick and tired." Confessing that we no longer want to allow our feelings to control us eventually leads us to the next discovery, hope.

Hope is where we begin to take control again of our feelings and our lives. Our natural response during a crisis is to lose control. We panic and lose sense of time. In order to combat this disarray, we overly-organize our lives as a form of sustaining ourselves. Often, those in grief will need friends, family, ministers, and others to help provide this organization. The key to this process is eventually developing an organized thought pattern that culminates with recovery and the beginnings of hope. The key to coming to a healing understanding that leads to hope is to organize our outward environment to the point where it becomes a model for the inward reorganization of our feelings.

However, at this point in our model, it's important to realize that one may go through the worst before it gets better. Depression, and the accompanying physical distress, is therefore our next stage in the model.

Depression

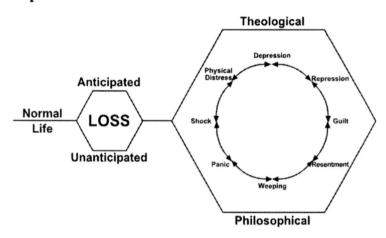

TOWNS DIAGRAM© OF
NORMAL GRIEF PROCESS
Graphic 5

In the normal grief process, most people will eventually feel depressed (see Graphic 5). Depression is the saddening and lowering of our mental spirit brought about by an extreme difficulty or burden. It is the emotional state of dejection or despair and feelings of worthlessness, hopelessness and apprehension.

When we find ourselves in the depth of depression or despair, we often begin to feel that no one has ever had a loss as significant as ours. Consequently, a rift or separation between us and our family, friends, and even God may result. When this happens, we find ourselves thinking thoughts that we would have otherwise never have ventured. At one point in my deep sorrow, I felt that no one cared. I felt that God could have kept the death from happening if He would have wanted to do so, but He did not. Quite honestly, I was angry with Him and felt a sense of comfort in deciding on a worthy scapegoat. It is easy to get such a persecution complex when we are depressed.

Frequently, depression occurs when someone we love is taken away from us. One of the most beneficial things we can do for someone depressed in such grief is to stand by him or her in quiet confidence and assure the person that "this too shall pass." The bereaved will probably resist such initial attempts for comfort, but as the length and intensity of the depression lessens, he or she develops a fuller appreciation for those supporters.

For some people, the depression clouds seem to dissipate rather quickly. For others, it may take weeks, months, or perhaps years before any new rays of light penetrate their downtrodden exterior. If the latter situation prevails, it is highly possible that physical distress will occur.

Let me say a word about depression medication. If one is unable to process heavy emotions, even with appropriate family support, I am not against seeking medical help, including medication or anti-depressants. Grief can affect our body chemistry, creating a state of disequilibrium that can often only be addressed through medication used to restore equilibrium. In Part Three, we will discuss a Life Quotients Formula that explains the idea of disequilibrium more thoroughly.

Physical Distress

Physical distress is the endurance of physical pain and symptoms of illness due to the grief process (see Graphic 5). Many people become physically ill because of an unresolved grief situation such as that posed by a personal loss. Unless these individuals can somehow resolve these emotional conflicts relative to the normal grief process, they may possibly continue to exhibit physical symptoms. Notice I said *resolve* not *solve*. We must resolve ourselves into acceptance and adjustment.

Thus, the depressing emotions of a person's mind and personality can physically compromise his or her body. The Bible astutely describes this phenomenon this way, "For as he thinks in his heart, so is he" (Proverbs 23:7).

Some of the physical symptoms of this distress may occur in the following manner:

- A feeling of tightness in the throat
- Choking with shortness of breath
- An incessant need for sighing
- An empty feeling in the abdomen
- Lack of muscular power
- An intensive distress described as "tension"

As mentioned prior, a person who is in the grief process may be plagued with dreams depicting horrible episodes surrounding the death of the loved one. In addition to the mental energy drained during these episodes, these dreams may cause physical distress that may drain a person's physical energy for hours and even days. This kind of physical and mental distress is normal. After a while, however, hope and acceptance may slowly emerge.

Hope-Acceptance

Hope is the resolve to expect the next stage in our model—a new, comfortable and somewhat normal life (refer back to Graphic 2). In this new life, we need to express our emotions. We still very much need encouragement from others. We do not hope for the possibilities of the old life returning— the comfortable and meaningful normal life we had before our loss. The past is gone. Life will never again be the same, as we once knew it with our loved one. However, there can be a new, normal life.

Sadly, some people take an attitude of shutting out possibilities for a new and meaningful normal life. When I experienced deep sorrow for the first time, I felt that I would never be happy again. Nothing could ever possibly ease the intensity of my heartache. I was unaware that it was normal to feel that way for extended periods. I didn't yet realize that hope lies only in acceptance of a situation. We can't find peace and hope in forgetting, in resignation, or in busyness but rather in some form of acceptance.

You may ask, "But how do I accept something that I don't want to accept?" Are you willing to let go of your human, self-focused motives and trust God in His sovereignty? If the answer is no, then keep praying for a willingness to be willing. Acceptance is a quiet resolution that comes slowly.

Relating to others will also help to alleviate loneliness. When you do not relate to others, you may become suspicious and disoriented. Continuing to relate to people will help you maintain a healthy sense of reality. You become mentally healthier when you stop denying the loss and unwanted change in your life and seek to make something constructive out of your experience.

Continued attempts to upgrade your level of understanding regarding grief will also provide invaluable coping assistance. Rather than casually accepting what others may have told you, use your experience to question, explore, and resolve conflicts forced upon you in your loss. You will not become reoriented by magic. You must *choose* to depend on courage and determination to find a new normal life without your loved one.

One of my friends put it this way, "When my

husband died, he did not ask me to go with him—so I have decided not to go!" Her spirit reveals that there is a choice, and she was choosing to keep on living life even though she no longer has her husband by her side. She started celebrating *her* life, rather than *their* life.

Finally, decide to be realistic in your hope. Take one day at a time. Recognize your needs and set realistic limits. As you become more realistic, you may decide to become part of a support system in order to share your grief. As you grow in hope and acceptance, you may find yourself providing counsel to others. Who knows? Your experience may be the turning point in someone else's healing process. Remember, resolution and hopeful determination, not tears, ultimately make grief more bearable.

God's Word Is Hope

People of faith do not suddenly achieve this state of compliance, although their beliefs and God's presence among and within them will help them tremendously. People of great faith grieve deeply over loss just as most everyone does. However, eventually they do understand that all is not lost, and they wish to experience life once again.

In the midst of grief, the Lord is not to be the

source of grief but the Great Sustainer in the midst of grief. He is our hope. This biblical truth is penned so eloquently in Lamentations 3:22–23, "The unfailing love of the LORD never ends! By his mercies we have been kept from complete destruction. Great is his faithfulness; his mercies begin afresh each day" (NLT). The ancient author was more impressed that God remained during grief than he was focused on trying to blame the grief on God.

Remember, hope is ultimately based on faith in God's unchanging Word—the only reliable foundation in our lives. "Jesus Christ is the same yesterday, today, and forever," Hebrews 13:8. Though we continue to struggle, we can find a new, normal life. The struggle is harder if we try to do it on our own. Relax and take God at His Word, regardless of how you feel right now.

Questions to Consider

The following questions are provided for individual reflection and/or group discussion. You may wish to work through these questions all at once or perhaps one at a time. Above all, consider them at your own pace. You might wish to journal your reflections on these questions as part of a meditation time or talk about them with a trusted family member or friend in quiet conversation. Some might use the material as part of a recovery group format. However you choose to use this feature of the book, spend time reflecting on each question as it relates to your recovery process.

1. Give examples of how it's possible to experience grief's "double-edged sword." (One side is grief and the other is relief.)

2. Describe where you are in the stages of the grief process (if you're still in the grieving process). If you've experienced the grieving process in the past, how did you respond in each stage? How long did each stage last? Any particular order?

a. Shock.

b. Panic.

c. Weeping.

d. Resentment-Anger.

e. Guilt.

f. Repression.

g. Depression.

h. Physical Distress.

i. Hope-Acceptance.

3. Are there other stages you have experienced that were not listed? Explain.

4. Which aspect of grief are you predominantly experiencing?

5. In what ways have you experienced some comfort as you realized that your grief is **not** abnormal?

6. What will you do as result of better understanding the normal grief process?

Part Three

Questions and Answers about Death and Grief

This reference section is designed to provide practical answers to perplexing questions about life, death, loss and grief. It is broad in scope, drawing on my many years of experience in dealing with those undergoing crises, and addresses some of the more common questions people often ask me.

Of course, change is part of the human condition. Changes and crises are to be expected from the "womb to the tomb"—no one escapes these basic characteristics of life. Although they vary from person to person, all crises require courage and discipline to overcome them. Change that produces positive effects does not lead to a deeper crisis. However, negative change usually produces seeds for questions and doubts that over time lead to disorganization and frustration. It is my hope that these answers will provide some instruction and comfort in order to help avoid further prolonged disruptions in life.

CHAPTER SIX

Preparing for Death

Question:
How can I prepare for my own death?

Most people‚ who attend a funeral or become associated with death entertain direct and indirect thoughts like, "Someday I am going to die.... Someday that will be me." As a result, one is forced to come to grips with the feelings and fears about one's own death. It is normal to feel anxious about our own future death. Even so, death is an event for which we must be prepared.

How are you directly or indirectly preparing for death? The question is more than, "How are you preparing for your loved ones' deaths?" It is also, "How are you preparing for your own?" We are going to be dead much longer than we will be alive on earth, so we had better plan toward eternity.

When I think about my own death, several areas help me to evaluate how well I am prepared for my death date. I invite you to evaluate these areas as well.

- Are you living in a right relationship with God? Have you committed yourself to God in terms of His role as the Leader (as Lord) and Forgiver (as Savior) in your life?

- Are you living in right relationship with your family, friends, and associates? Are there any relationships that need reconciliation and repair? Have you learned to disagree without being disagreeable? Are you enjoying people?

- Are you investing your life in things that will last for eternity? Or have you committed your life to things that will perish when you die?

One day, you will have to face your own death. There is much that you can do to prepare for it, and now is the time to settle these matters. Of course, life must be more than waiting to die and merely existing on earth. Life is for living! Perhaps the prayer of Saint Francis of Assisi should be the pattern for our lives so that in death we will have no regrets:

Lord, make me an instrument of your peace
Where there is hatred...let me sow love
Where there is injury...pardon
Where there is doubt...faith
Where there is despair...hope
Where there is darkness...light
Where there is sadness...joy
O Divine Master, grant that I may not so much
     seek
To be consoled...as to console
To be understood...as to understand

To be loved…as to love
For, it is in giving…that we receive,
It is in pardoning…that we are pardoned.
It is in dying…that we are born to eternal life.

-St. Francis of Assisi- (c. 1181-1226)

Question:
What are the stages of grief that a dying person may experience?

It is helpful to understand how dying people go through several rational and emotional stages in their process of dying. Dr. Elizabeth Kubler-Ross has described the stages the dying person experiences.[i] Her work has become a primary resource for professionals and lay people working in the field of death and dying. Since most people who work in this area use the Kubler-Ross outline, let's look at these stages in order.

1. Denial and isolation. When a person receives the initial diagnosis that he or she has a terminal illness, a typical first reaction is one of disbelief or denial. Denial is a temporary defense mechanism. It serves as a necessary buffer, a delay against the overwhelming anxiety until the person can deal with the news. The person usually says things such as, "Oh, no! This cannot be true!" or "There must be a mistake!" He or she doesn't believe the medical reports and insists on repeat examinations. Often, the person begins to solicit another doctor's medical opinion.

During the time of denial, there is an intense feeling of isolation from loved ones, friends, and from the real world. Those giving care must wait through this first phase and let the person know that they are available and willing to listen when he or she desires to talk. If a dying person denies his or her illness for a prolonged time, even in spite of advancing symptoms, those who must care for the person should give compassion and support as death comes closer. Extensive denial is unhealthy because it hinders the dying person's preparations to face the inevitable separation and grief. Yet, some people maintain their denial to the end. Denial is usually interrupted by the next stage, anger.

2. Anger. As anger rises, the patient goes through periods of rage, envy, and resentment. This second phase begins when the reality of the prognosis is established. The feelings of anger are usually displaced onto things or people. One might hear him or her say things like, "The doctor is no good," "This hospital is terrible," "Nurses are neglectful," or "Nobody cares." The family and health-care professionals usually withstand the worst of all this anger, but it can include ministers, and even God. No one, it seems, can do anything right to please the dying person, and he or she becomes angry with all those who go on living.

Many questions arise in the midst of a person's anger. The major question is a belligerent, "Why me?" This stage is very difficult to handle by medical professionals and the family. The dying person is not actually angry at other people. He is angry at death and the fact of his or her dying. Anger may be present with the awareness of dying, but it can continue as long as the person has made no satisfactory resolution to death.

Anger has to be expressed, and for the dying person, it may eventually pass. The dying person's anger must not be taken personally A calm approach is needed to help lower anger and anxiety, which usually ushers in the feelings of the next stage, bargaining.

3. Bargaining. The third stage is bargaining,

either conscious or unconscious, expressed to others through direct or indirect behavior. The dying person tries to enter into some kind of agreement in order to postpone death. Bargaining usually consists of promises to God, doctors, and family. The dying patient says something like this to God, "If You will let me live, then I will serve You." "If You heal me, I will read the Bible." He or she may say to the doctors, "I will be a good patient if you will help me to get well. Promise me that I have another year to live." To the family, he or she says, "I will do (this or that) if you will help me to live."

It is important during this time to note any underlying feelings of guilt or regrets the dying person may have about his or her life. We should listen to those expressions of regret and grief. During this time, we can help the dying person to become more realistic in his or her feelings. As Dr. Kubler-Ross shows, a patient cannot keep the bargaining promises—like a little child who naively promises, "I will be good forever." Needless to say, the child gets into trouble the next day, thereby breaking the promise. This realization often leads to the next stage, depression.

4. Depression. When the patient realizes that

bargaining won't help to sustain health, the patient usually goes into a time of depression. During this time, dying people grieve over the loss of body image, his or her role in life, relationships, and financial losses. Then he or she begins the grief of separating from life itself.

There are two major types of depression. Reactive depression is the sudden response to a great number of problems that a patient faces. First, there is the shock of everything coming at once. Then there is preparatory depression, the normal grief the patient has to go through in order to prepare to separate from this world. The initial reaction many people have to someone's depression is to try to cheer him or her up. This may meet the needs of the caring person but not the dying person's needs.

At this point, the patient is not denying his or her inevitable approach to death. He or she is trying to "put it all together" and find personal meaning. This usually brings about the fifth stage of the grief process, acceptance.

5. Acceptance. The dying person usually comes to this stage if given enough time and help. Unless there is an unexpected, sudden death, all the stages may be completed. During this final stage, a patient may tend to separate from all of his or her relationships. During this time, the person's focus is making his or her own preparations for death.

Acceptance is not necessarily defined as a happy stage. The patient does not say, "Great. I'm going to die." Instead, there may be very little emotion expressed, since this last stage is almost void of emotional feeling. Communication becomes more nonverbal than verbal. Acceptance takes the form of resignation, and the patient seems ready to die with dignity. The famous statement by columnist, Stewart Alsop, "A dying person needs to die like a sleepy person needs to sleep," has perhaps best described it.

With acceptance, the cycle of stages in the process of dying moves toward completion. Yet, the process of dying is too complicated to put such simplistic labels on a cycle. Not every dying person will experience all of these stages or in the order presented here. Yet, these five stages are usually the natural, normal progression in the life of a dying person.

At the end of these stages, when it has become clear to a person that he or she is dying and that death is inevitable, two major issues need to be faced. First, the dying person needs to receive permission from the significant people left behind to leave. Loved ones should not attempt to make a dying person feel that his or her death is so unacceptable that it will take away all meaning and purpose from their lives. The dying person needs to know that life will somehow go on for the ones left behind. Second, the dying person needs to release every significant person and possession voluntarily. It is always better to have the feeling of surrendering gracefully those things we know we cannot keep rather than maintaining the attitude that they are being "snatched away" from us. Thus, peace ideally characterizes the completion of these stages.

Question:
What are the stages of anticipatory or pregrieving that survivors may experience prior to a loss?

A growing number of people in a specific category have to deal with long term, terminal illness and the span of time before the person actually dies. Several situations fit into this category. The most predominant currently ranges from Alzheimer's to cancer.

The family and caregivers are all subject to pregrieving. However, several variables determine the depth or intensity of that grief.

Relationship

First, the relationship with the dying person is a factor. If the relationship is intimate, there will naturally be a deeper grief.

Temperament

Second, the survivor's personality temperament is another factor regarding the intensity of grief. We respond to circumstances based on our personality type or temperament. This one factor may be as or more significant than any other. Every human personality has a combination of characteristics. How we behave or function in a crisis may often be the result of our own peculiar combination of characteristics. Our attitudes—born of these characteristics—greatly influence our approach and response to life and death.

The classic Greek and Roman philosophers, as well as contemporary writers, have categorized these characteristics into "temperaments." Tim LaHaye has probably done as much as anyone to familiarize America with the classic concepts of four personality temperaments.[ii] Most people seem to be dominated by characteristics in one temperament and are strongly influenced by traits in a second or third type. Let's look at the four examples in order to further our understanding of pregrieving.

- The first temperament is called *sanguine*, best represented by the extroverted optimist. He or she is lively and emotional, warm and optimistic. By nature, this person is friendly, has a pleasant personality and has a "happy time" entertaining people. The sanguine is at his or her best when he or she is the life of the party. The sanguine is never at a loss for words and is often envied by many people who are less extroverted. People with this temperament make good entertainers, salespersons, social workers, actors, and speakers.

  The sanguine is also adaptable, doesn't fight reality, is easy going, enjoys life, is good-natured, and doesn't get overwrought. Of all the temperaments, this one will likely respond best in crises. Persons of this temperament thrive on situations where the outcome is not known, where there is freedom to test the limits. Therefore, this person would probably find humor in the situation even in the process of dying.

• The second temperament is the *melancholic*, best symbolized by an introvert prone to pessimism. He or she is extremely selective, analytical, and thorough concerning life. As a deep thinker, his or her idealism tends to exaggerate the negative. Therefore, the melancholic is a perfectionist with a sensitive, emotional nature. He or she will find a great deal of meaning in life and death from some form of personal sacrifice. This person is a faithful friend and has a deep appreciation for aesthetics.

Some believe the melancholy temperament has the greatest strengths. Yet, it also has some of the largest potential weaknesses. He or she may be subject to moodiness, self-centeredness, rigidity, and vengefulness. The melancholic will be dependable, painstaking, thorough, competent, hard working, patient, persevering, sensible, and stable. However, even the most cursory glance at a melancholic will detect a thread of pessimism coloring all he or she does. Above all else, this person feels he or she must be prepared. Many of his or her actions will be preparing for those setbacks and untoward events that are bound to occur. The melancholic is not just gloomily foretelling calamity and disaster; rather, he or she is setting something aside for rainy days. Murphy's Laws such as, "Whatever can go wrong will" or "Everything takes longer and costs more than expected" could have been composed by a melancholic. Therefore, a melancholic may fear and resist change in the dying process, though he or she knows what is happening.

- Third is the *choleric*, best typified by a strong-willed, hard-driving person. He or she is prone to be enthusiastic, insightful, creative, imaginative, and empathetic. This person will do well as a researcher, teacher, counselor, writer, or psychologist and displays a hot, quick, active, practical temperament. Usually the *choleric* is self-sufficient and independent as he or she sets super-high goals and works tirelessly to achieve them. It is easy for this person to make decisions for people. Since the choleric thrives on activities, adversities only serve as encouragement.

Unfortunately, his or her response to a pending death can fall into a pattern of anticipation, accompanied by a considerable investment of effort and emotion, ending in disappointment over what could have been that was not. Some of this disenchantment is born of unrealistic expectations. Persons with a choleric temperament work toward a vision of perfection and, of course, nothing ever lives up to the magnificence of its conception. Therefore, they can be unreasonably demanding on both themselves and others around them.

- Fourth is the *phlegmatic* temperament represented by a slow, good-natured person. He or she is calm, cool, well balanced, and has an easy-going temperament. This person is happy, unexcitable, pleasant, and avoids excessive involvement as much as possible. This person never is ruffled, regardless of circumstances and seldom shows great emotion. As this person keeps his or her emotions under control, the phlegmatic also enjoys a dry sense of humor, often keeping people in "stitches" and never cracking a smile. He or she is a big teaser who delights in poking fun at other temperaments. He or she makes a good accountant, diplomat, scientist, teacher, leader, or a technician who is meticulous.

Phlegmatic persons are abstract, analytical, curious, efficient, exacting, independent, ingenious, systematic, and inventive. It is important to them to be able to understand, control, predict, and explain reality. They feel a tremendous need to be and to appear competent and capable of handling whatever occurs. This is the most self-critical of the four temperaments. They badger themselves about their errors, tax themselves with a resolve to improve, and ruthlessly monitor their own progress. Therefore, the stress associated with an anticipated death can cause a phlegmatic to become tense and compulsive. Self-doubt can also be a side effect. The danger is that he or she will be so inhibited by self-doubt that his or her resolve will fade.

According to personality temperament theories, most people are dominated by characteristics of one temperament and are strongly influenced by traits in a second or third type. A study of the four temperaments will enable you to examine yourself, determine your strengths and weaknesses, and understand why you react to the impending death of someone.

Value Set and Belief System

Third, the survivor's value set and belief system can also determine the depth of the grief experience. For example, there are several inadequate, immature, and even unscriptural concepts of God. Some perceive God as a "slot machine in the sky" into which one puts money, pulls the "prayer lever," and awaits the payoff of escaping the impending death. Others view God as a giant computer that people feed their problems into for automatic answers.

Another inadequate concept of God is that He is a spiritual Santa Claus with a sack full of gifts to give to those who have been "good." The assumption is that if a person lives right, then only good things will happen to him or her.

One of the most damaging concepts people have about God is that of a policeman who keeps people in line. They believe God is watching and hoping they will mess up so He can crack them over the head with a billy club.

Perhaps the most common misconception people have is that God is an impersonal, formal

Sunday event. In other words, God is only to be worshiped through ritual and form, organ music and a sermon.

It is imperative that Christians have a scriptural concept of God. It is impossible to have a healthy relationship with God without having a scriptural understanding of who He is. An inadequate concept of God will bring about a wrong response to Him and a distorted relationship with Him. On the other hand, a scriptural idea of God will build a healthy relationship with Him based on truth.

Scripture reveals God as the trinity of Father, Son, and Spirit. Throughout time, God has been revealing Himself. Scripture gives a progressive revelation of His nature and ways. Therefore, one's faith and values are strong factors as to how they may pregrieve a loss even before it happens.

Circumstances

A fourth strong factor of anticipatory or pregrieving is the method or circumstances of the death. If it is an extended prolonged span of time in the dying process, the family and caregivers may experience a depletion of body, mind, emotions, will, and spirit— all components of the Life Quotients Formula we will study later in this section.

Another factor is the intensity of pain experienced by the dying. Their attitude is also a determining factor as to how survivors pregrieve.

When a family member or friend realizes that a loved one is going to die, the surviving person may experience several feelings. A dear friend shared with me some insights on anticipatory grief. Carolyn Roberts, Ph.D., a licensed Marriage and Family Therapist in Los Angeles, has summarized them below. [iii]

1. *Recognition that the problem won't go away.*
   As denial fades and reality moves in, survivors realize they are probably in for a long, extended experience.

2. *Readiness for the roller coaster to stop.*
   The good, bad, and even worst days wear on the survivors. This may result in the survivor silently desiring that the process quickly take its course. The extreme high and low emotions are so depleting.

3. *Remorse that the other person has to die for it to stop.*
   Survivors usually feel great guilt about the

fact that the only way this situation will conclude is for the loved one to die.

4. *Reluctance to let someone go.*

The survivors may start to feel that the "bad" days with the dying are better than living without the loved one. It is extremely difficult for most people to say goodbye.

5. *Releasing the individual who is ill and detaching so you can go on.*

The survivor needs to come to a place where he or she can release the dying and "give permission" for the dying to die.

6. *Relief at the end.*

As we've stated, grief is a double-edged sword. On one side of the sword is the grief that the person died. The other side is relief that it is completed. Usually there is a pseudo guilt associated with this relief.

7. *Resolving grief.*

When the death actually happens, the survivors may realize that their pregrieving was not enough to process the loss completely. The "cold facts" of grief grip the survivors. At this point, the survivors probably go through the normal grief process. We do not get over grief; we learn to live with it. This is where the method of resolving grief comes into focus. One must admit, vent, and release grief in order to find resolve in the loss.

8. *Regrieving at significant times.*

Although survivors may feel that they have resolved their grief, there may come a time that certain identifications with the loss may cause them to regrieve the death. Illustrations of this might be the anniversary of the death as well as significant calendar dates and experiences.

Question:

How can I deal with my fears concerning death?

In dealing with the fear of death, the question of cause and effect confronts us. Some might say that the relationship between these two variables is reciprocal, as is the avoidance and anxiety we experience when contemplating our own death.

This lack of a definitive approach to the above question affords varying levels and types of fear surrounding death. In observance of this predicament, the following examines the greatest fears about death that occur during the developmental stages of life: [iv]

Teens:
Not marrying
Not becoming a parent
Not having enough time to become a professional

Twenties:
Leaving family
How loved ones would cope with grief

Thirties:
Female:
Abandonment of children
Guilt feelings
Not living to see children grown
Male:
Financial security for family
End of productivity

Loss of control

Forties:
Welfare of spouse
Welfare of children
Financial security of survivors
Dread of separation

Fifties:
Welfare of family
Welfare of children
Welfare of grandchildren
Anxiety about extended suffering
Fear of the process of dying

Sixties, Seventies, Eighties:
Welfare of families
Fear of being kept alive beyond hope of recovery
Fear of loss of control of estate

We all have fears and anxieties about approaching the unknown, especially death. Ironically, there is usually a greater fear of the process of dying than of death itself. Even so, we can do several things to overcome our fears about death and/or dying:

1. <u>We must realize that we cannot escape death</u>. By accepting our impending death as a fact, we can neutralize the demoralizing and paralyzing fears. When we have a clear understating of this fact, acceptance comes easier without false hopes or bitterness, and we really start living.

2. <u>After accepting the inevitability of death, we can become courageous, decisive, and live with less fear</u>. We must assume a total plan for life, one that will help us to understand that facing up to death leads to strength. To accept the inevitability of death means to take charge of one's life.

3. <u>When we accept the fact that we will die, we waste no time finding meaning and fulfillment in life</u>. When we live life fully, we fear death least and love life most.

CHAPTER SEVEN

Grief Management

Question:
How can I get through the holiday seasons?

Grief does not take a holiday during special occasions. Christmas, birthdays, anniversaries and other significant calendar dates seem to be a time when grief emerges quite heavily.

Several situations tend to cause a greater depth of grief when the past is too well remembered. It is easy to idealize the past as perfect more than realistic. Thinking about the losses can lead to a deeper depression. An obsession with the event may be cause for greater loneliness. Unrealistic expectations may also compound grief. The overexertion physically, emotionally, as well as financially that is often associated with the holiday season can also contribute to one's grief. It is wise for the bereaved to understand the basic survival needs such as food, rest, sleep, and exercise are not to be ignored. Do not turn grief and anger inward and punish yourself by ignoring such necessities.

It is also wise to anticipate the needs of the holidays or special occasions. When such times approach, the major task is to set realistic goals and limits for yourself, family, and friends. The following questions will provide some helpful hints as you decide what is comfortable for everyone concerned:

1. Will we talk openly about the deceased loved one?

2. Who will take responsibility for the family activities or festivities?

3. Will we keep the family traditions or change the holiday routine?

4. Will we decorate for the season?

If the needs of the season are not anticipated, there will probably be a great deal of regrieving. This may bring on painful thinking as well as frustration and anger. There may be a sad physical countenance and physical symptoms such as digestive problems, irregular heartbeat, headaches, tension, and general regrieving.

Further assistance for alleviating grief will be afforded if you decide to do something for someone else during the season. Give money in memory of your loved one. Adopt a needy family for the holidays. Invite a guest to share the season. Get involved in a service project.

These activities help you stop and smell the roses of the holiday season and help you realize the joy that comes in giving. You cannot "out give" God. He will ensure your generosity will come back to you in a more meaningful way!

Question Four:
How can I help someone in the grief process?

Most people start by telephoning those experiencing grief, going in person to see them, sending flowers or giving money to their favorite charity. You may invite them over to your home once or twice to prove that you care. However, most likely, you may soon slip quietly back into your own routine assuring yourself that you have extended all manner of condolence and offers for assistance. This, however, is not enough!

Persons in grief need you desperately. To help them effectively demands an understanding of the grief process, a willingness to listen, and a substantial amount of time. Become involved in their lives and help with any areas where they may require assistance. Above all else, be genuine in communicating your sincerity and concern.

Quite often, the funeral is not the end of the grief process—only the beginning. Let the grieving persons express their feelings after its completion. You may not particularly want to hear the painful content of what they say, but they need to vent such anguish to someone. Merely listening can provide needed comfort. In other words, you may not want to hear it, but they need to say it to someone who cares! One of the most meaningful strategies for helping people during the grief process is to encourage them to keep lives in proper balance. The most effective way is to treat each quotient of our lives as significant.

The following "Life Quotients Formula" is an important tool for achieving such equilibrium:

Life Quotients Formula

$$Life = Bq + Iq + Eq + Wq + Sq$$

Bq   Body quotient (Physical: bodily needs)
    Nutrition   - food
    Exercise   - physical workout
    Rest   - sleep

Iq   Intelligence quotient (Mind: thinking and reasoning)
    Nutrition   - reading
    Exercise   - problem solving
    Rest   - meditating

Eq   Emotional quotient (Emotions: personality and feelings)

Nutrition - process
Exercise - control
Rest - quiet

Wq Willpower quotient (Choice: choosing to make choices)
Nutrition - think
Exercise - commitment
Rest - relax

Sq Spiritual quotient (Faith: belief system)
Nutrition - Scripture
Exercise - practice
Rest - abide

The Life Quotients Formula is an attempt to bring balance into our lives. If one quotient is deficient, there is a systemic reaction in the total. For example, when our Emotional quotient (Eq) has disequilibrium, it diminishes the other quotients. If our Willpower quotient (Wq) is negatively affected, then it affects all choices in the areas of life or the grief process. Since our Spiritual quotient (Sq) is the foundational focus of life, a deficiency in this area gives the sense that "nothing else seems work right." Therefore, as we take proper care of the quotients of our life, we will resolve our grief more readily. Disequilibrium in any one of the quotients may cause a prolonged grief process.

Question:
What can I say to someone in grief?

In every grief situation, many people often say something to the effect, "If there is anything I can do, let me know." Although the persons who make such an offer mean well, it often proves a shallow communication effort with little intent for action. We must realize that most bereaved individuals will not pick up the phone and say, "I'm taking you up on your offer." Thus, it might prove necessary for us to initiate the first move.

It would be interesting if we could know what Adam said to Eve and vice versa on the day of their son Abel's funeral. However, a more probing question is in regards to what they said to each other a day later. Or a month later? Or the next year? Even a decade later? Whatever the content of such conversation, they somehow coped in dealing with the death of their son.

Similar grief and attempts for coping through

verbal comfort have plagued generations since that infamous time. In many ways, what you *do not* say is as important as what you *do* say. Indeed, many messages produce more harm than good. The following negative clichés demonstrate this notion and provide a guide to individuals as to what *not* to say to those who have experienced personal loss:

What to Avoid:

1. "I know just how you feel." No, you do not! You know how *you* felt in a similar situation, but you do not know how another person feels. You are motivated by kindness, but if you say those words, you may cause alienation and uncomfortable feelings. Do not assume or presume. If there is similarity in the grief that you have experienced, let the one who is currently grieving be the one to mention or claim your wisdom.

2. "How are you?" This social greeting is usually considered surface. When asked of a grieving person, it is like a buzz saw cutting into his or her emotions. If the bereaved person were honest, he or she would probably reply, "Oh, quite devastated by my loss, thank you." If you

truly desire to know how people feel, listen to them. If you really listen to people, they will tell you how they are feeling!

3. "<u>Time will heal.</u>" This is the truth. It will. It does. Yet, do not say this to the rawness of new sorrow. When you articulate such a cliché, you imply that the deceased will not always be as important to the survivor as he or she is right now. The person will probably feel the need to afford you the following animated response, "Do *not* say that!" It may be true, but it adds to the agony now.

4. "<u>I pity you in this situation.</u>" The grieving do not want your pity! They desire love, compassion, and understanding but not pity. Your pity will probably induce self-pity for the bereaved. This will only further erode that person's spirit.

5. "<u>If there is anything I can do...</u>" The one in sorrow usually proves unable to discern adequate responses to such a statement. Your appropriate action would be to analyze the situation and determine what needs to be done. Then, offer to do the specifics that you are capable of assum-

ing. Take the initiative. Do not ask hollow questions. Instead, take care of immediate needs.

Let's shift our attention now to specific actions you *should* take when interacting with the bereaved. The following are some suggestions that should prove positive and meaningful to the grieving recipient:

What to Do:

1. <u>Take some initiatives</u>. Do not wait to be asked to help. Look around and analyze the situation. Determine what you can do to assist immediately and ultimately. And do it!

2. <u>Listen to the grieving</u>. Perhaps this is the most important thing that you can do. During the total grief process—from beginning through readjustment—listen, listen, listen! Listen without heavy advising or lecturing. Listen with quiet inquiries at appropriate times. One of my friends put it this way, "Grief wants to be heard." It not only wants to be heard; it needs to be heard. A great deal of theological and philosophical reevaluation needs to be heard from most grieving people. Above

all, be a long term listener. Listen on the first day, through the first six months, and perhaps even after a year. Do not be afraid of your silence as you listen to a bereaved person.

3. <u>Say what you deeply feel when it is appropriate</u>. Many people who seek to give comfort are timid in saying what they deeply feel. Be honest and simple in your statements, and the grieving will genuinely appreciate you. It is not only important to say it person-to-person but also by telephone. It is also very meaningful to email and write notes and letters periodically. Above all, communicate what you are feeling!

4. <u>Keep in touch</u>. Expressions of sympathy demonstrated through flowers, cards, and food are most appreciated in the beginning. Later on, however, most people tend to get busy and forget the grieving. Remembering in the days, months, or perhaps years that follow may be even more helpful and healing than your initial contacts. I do not remember much *what* others said to me when I was in deep sorrow, but I do remember *who* comforted me during that time. Particularly memorable are those who maintained contact

with me throughout my grief continuum.

Remember, do not say anything negative or disrespectful to those enduring the burden of grief. The most important thing is to communicate the availability of your presence and assistance. One of the most meaningful notes that I ever received was from a student in one of my classes who lost his father. The note simply read, "Your attitude of 'I care' was a deep comfort me." Simple, yet poignant wording.

Grief behavior may take different forms. It may take the form of facing up to what has happened, or it may result from problems caused by the blockage of bottled-up feelings. Either way, expression of grief is a therapeutic part of managing his or her experience. Some of the following ideas may assist you in implementing a much-needed strategy in grief management.

When the grieving person gets "sick and tired of being sick and tired," these factors become extremely important to his or her progress. At that point, you may want to encourage the grieving person to:

1. ADMIT IT!

You must admit to yourself what has happened in the death situation. Boldly say aloud, "My loved one is dead because of_____ (fill in the blank)." In other words, call the person by name and admit he or she is deceased.

2. VENT IT!

After you have admitted to yourself why your loved one died, then tell others how you feel about your loss. Get your feelings out. I encourage you to talk, cry, scream—just get your deep, emotional feelings out of your system. Perhaps the grief is prolonged because you are trying to get "things" back to the way they were. Since this is not possible, release your feelings.

3. RELEASE IT!

After you have admitted to yourself and others how you feel about your loss, release your feelings. To release feelings means to open up and turn them over to God. Then release your loved one. Give him or her permission to be deceased and present with God until you join your loved one again. Also, give yourself permission to enjoy living on earth until that time.

Finding a new normal life without the deceased is a deeply personal journey. Perhaps these four statements will aid as you bring some closure to your loss.

I continue to love you! This relationship was extremely meaningful to you. There will always be a special love for that person.

Thank you! This relationship contributed greatly to your life. It helped to make you the person that you are. You are deeply appreciative of all his or her contributions to your life.

I forgive you. Regardless of how wonderful a relationship was, some degrees of resentment or anger likely wounded the relationship at one time or another. In the case of suicide, resentment is almost certain, as our loved one took his or her life away from us. Therefore, choose to forgive any infraction that hurt you. As a result, it becomes easier to capitalize on the positive aspects of the relationship.

Goodbye. Although the relationship will always be a part of your life, the door of access to the person has been closed. No one can ever take his or her place, yet new places may be created if you desire.

Grief brings about the painful reality that we do not know how to live until we know how to die! In the process of learning how to live and die, certain factors about our behavior are frightening but normal. If we treat our normal feelings of grief as if they were abnormal, our mind short-circuits; thus, guilt and frustration result. I cannot stress enough how important it is that we treat normal human feelings normally!

Most importantly, you may find power in faith that you did not realize was there until you put Scripture to work in your life. You will find a faith stronger than death! Because you now have some deeper insights into the normal grief process, you will be better able to communicate with a person in grief about your faith and about the process of death and dying.

Question:
How can I deal with loneliness?

Those who are grieving often experience an

internal war between aloneness and loneliness. There is a vast difference between these two conditions. All of us need time where we can be *alone* to reassess values, establish priorities, and develop a sense of direction. Yet who wants to experience *loneliness*? No one does.

Loneliness occurs when a person lacks the inner resources to be alone. In other words, loneliness is a longing for companionship or feelings of isolation and despair brought on by losing a relationship.

While it is true that no one ever takes the place of anyone else; yet there are new places created. We must learn to use aloneness and deal with loneliness.

There is a dynamic, positive aspect of loneliness! It can cause us to want to establish (or re-establish) a right relationship with others. When we are alone, we have the opportunity to do some very important things such as:

- <u>Reflect</u>. Rethink about what has happened to us and meditate. We can review our life constructively.

- <u>Evaluate</u>. We can take advantage of the

opportunity to sort out facts and feelings and to determine what is going on in our life.

- Grow. We have a chance to go through the decision-making process, considering different alternatives and their probable consequences. This kind of objective reasoning provides a healthy format for personal growth. While we are engaging in these inner activities alone, we develop a deeper comprehension of the true meaning of life and relationships.

A person's self-concept and self-acceptance also play an important role in handling loneliness and using aloneness. The words of theologian Paul Tillich, come to my mind when I am talking with lonely people, "It is easy to be lonely, but it is difficult to be alone." Therefore, aloneness is the creative way of being alone and liking it. Loneliness is an undesired and unwelcome separation from other people. There are several helpful hints for resolving loneliness into aloneness:

1. Accept the fact that, at times, you are going

to be lonely. Recognize your feelings and deal with them.

2. <u>Realize that feelings of loneliness are not abnormal</u>. It is very normal for all people to be lonely at certain times.

3. <u>Learn to be still at times</u>. As you practice being still, your quiet-mindedness will help you to put your feelings into proper perspective. In other words, learn to develop inner peace.

4. <u>Learn that sharing loneliness helps to increase the enjoyment of aloneness</u>. When you are lonely, find an opportunity to relate to other lonely people. As you share your loneliness, you will discover that you are not as lonely as you thought you were.

5. <u>Remember there is a time for loneliness and a time for aloneness</u>. Do not be ashamed of the pain of dealing with the less desired state of loneliness.

CHAPTER EIGHT

General Questions about Grief and Death

Question:
How do I tell children about death?

Eventually, you will be in the position of needing to communicate with a child about death. It is important to note at such times that adults can play an integral role in yielding those of tender years a realistic yet meaningful philosophy and theology. However, when adults are experiencing distress due to personal loss, they often try to protect children from the knowledge and/or unsavory experiences afforded by death. However, the loss should be viewed as a family crisis time that is shared by all members of the family—even children.

The first exposure most children have to the words "dead" and "killed" is through television programming. Such verbal displays do not adequately prepare them for the reality of personal loss. The parent who is wise will gently and objectively discuss death before a family loss rather than relent to the manner constructed by a television network. The discovery of dying plants or a dead pet may provide the opportunity for such fundamental attempts at death education.

A child's reaction or response to death is usually influenced by at least three major factors: the family structure, the circumstances of the death, and the religious beliefs of the family. Grief is a process in which the family shares in a series of thoughts, feelings, and actions, during a period of adjustment to the loss of a loved one. If the family stays together and deals with grief successfully, the children will be able to cope better with their loss and confused bewilderment.

In order to help children, the parents and friends must communicate ideas that are rational and help-ful. A child should not, however, be told in detail the things that he or she cannot understand. Rather, parents should provide explanations modified to the child's level of understanding and maturation. Furthermore, parents should answer children's questions about death directly and honestly.

Although many adults have good intentions, some explanations of death may cause fear, doubt, and guilt rather than comfort. Realize that young children are forming their beliefs by what you tell them. Thus, the following are some negative perspectives to avoid when attempting to construct such explanations of death for children:

1. Stories and fairy tales about death.

2. Giving the child an explanation that you cannot accept yourself.

3. Interpretations that may backfire and cause the child to reach unintended conclusions.

Children should be told the truth. Many overprotective parents, in their haste to save their children from all unpleasant things, try to protect them from the pain and grief elicited by a death. Don't deprive children of their right to grieve. For example, it is more disturbing for them to think that their grandmother has left them to go live with God than for them to realize that she died from a disease she did not want and fought bravely to overcome.

When a death occurs and children are not told the truth about what happened, they may become confused. Anxiety may soon fill their mind, and they may fill the imposed knowledge gap with figments of their imagination far more bizarre than the truth could ever provide. Such childhood fantasies can be carried into maturity and perpetuate the inability to grasp the reality of death.

In communicating with children about death, it is of paramount importance to convey that death itself does not hurt. They must understand that the family and friends are weeping because of the sadness of losing a person who meant so much to them. Children, well known for their blatant honesty, often easily accept such frank expressions of grief afforded by the adult when they are relayed in comprehensible terms. Furthermore, such meticulously constructed admissions of grief can also help the adults in question face avoided issues regarding their own response to the death of a loved one.

Should children attend the funeral? Children should never be forced to attend a funeral; yet they should be encouraged. It can be a comforting experience for young children to attend the actual service. Therefore, give them a clear, detailed explanation in advance so they know what to expect during the event. They need to know the purpose of the funeral is to recognize the value of dignity regarding the deceased person's life. This will aid in encouraging survivors to express their honest feelings of disappointment and pain concerning their loss.

The presence of all the family and friends at the funeral service will help children to realize that they are not alone during this time. Following the funeral's completion, it is important to communicate to children that though we do not easily get over the loss of someone we loved, we have to learn to live with the fact of his or her death.

When sorrow is suppressed, it can cause distorted or delayed grief reactions. This can cause deep psychological injury to children as well as to adults. Children need understanding when they cannot comprehend their own feelings. They must have love, acceptance, and reassurance from adults who are near them. Children should not be encouraged to hold back the flow of tears. Tears are nature's way of reducing emotional pressure and washing grief away more quickly.

Feel free to talk about past experiences involving the deceased. This will cause the deceased to become an appropriate memory for children and allow them to direct their emotions and thoughts toward the living more easily.

Many adults need to take the word "death" off the taboo list and let it be discussed openly and meaningfully. The following ideas may be meaningful for most adults in guiding the conversation:

1. Talk about death when children want to talk about it.

2. Determine what children are really asking.

3. It can be more devastating to answer questions that have not been asked.

4. Answers should be honed and geared to the maturation level of the child.

5. Permit the child to go through the normal grief process.

Whether you find yourself as a parent, or a friend of children who are in sorrow, these ideas should better equip you to communicate with them concerning the issue of death. Since death is a certainty, we should not let children be unprepared for the inevitable grief it affords.

Question Nine:
What is the difference between suicide grief and general grief?

Up to this point, we have been discussing general grief. However, grief from suicide seems to have a different set of rules than the normal grief process. Victims of suicide grief carry a longer period of mourning than victims from other means of death.

One afternoon in my office, I listened to a college freshman cry out as he exclaimed, "I do not want either to live or die, but to do both at the same time—usually one more than the other." Tragically, this student decided one day that he wanted to die more than he wanted to live, even though the support community tried multiple strategies for preserving his life.

Death is the ultimate loss for humans. Most people spend their lives fleeing from death. To cause one's death intentionally is the ultimate abnormal life crisis. Tony Salvatore, a motivational speaker and professional counselor whose own son committed suicide, has been a great resource person for helping to understand aspects of suicide.[v] He granted permission to use the following adaptation of some of his ideas about what makes suicide different from other general grief:

1. Suicide is a death in which victims usually have anger towards the deceased.

2. While the signs of suicide may have been present for months, suicide is rarely expected—leaving no time for bereavement preparation.

3. Suicides are regarded as murders until proven otherwise. Questioning by law enforcement interrupts grieving.

4. Those left behind have likely shared in the

depression and/or problems that ultimately contributed to the act of suicide.

5. Survivors may deal with their own self-destructive impulses.

6. "Is suicide hereditary?" becomes a realistic question and fear for those left behind.

7. Those that discover the body are left to deal with highly traumatic visual images.

8. Suicide victims will always be tortured with the unanswered question, "If I had only done this, then…"

Experiencing a suicide loss is a disorienting and disruptive life experience. Unlike those who experience other traumatic losses, they are usually left to make sense of the loss alone. They may also be made to feel that what happened was the result of "something wrong" with the victim, or families, and are treated accordingly.

For those dealing with grief loss, the most difficult emotion is the feeling of rejection. In many ways, suicide is like divorce to a spouse, disowning to a child, and a failure to a parent. There is no road map to guide suicide grievers to a comforting destination; nor is there a schedule as to how long it may take us to get there.

The debate as to the primary causes of suicide continues, yet in almost every case, suicide appears to be preceded by vehement levels of psychological pain. The following list reveals significant insights concerning such pain:

1. Much of what has been learned about dealing with physical pain applies to psychache. Psychological pain is under-assessed and under-treated. More attention is paid to the causes than to pain itself. Suicide grievers are left to contend with pain alone.

2. Severe pain has the same impact both physically and psychologically. Anxiety, sleeplessness, fatigue, depression, and anger set in. These modify and aggravate the pain and elicit changes that increase stress (which further drives pain). Severe pain is destructive.

3. Worsening pain attacks self-control and self-

esteem. It generates fear and powerlessness and creates a sense of profound isolation.

4. Pain overwhelms coping and leaves helplessness in its wake.

5. Pain travels in the company of suffering, which has been defined as, "A state of severe distress induced by the loss of intactness of person or by a threat that the person believes will result in the loss of…intactness." Suffering is where pain and suicide meet.

6. Suicidal individuals and those with chronic pain share the same experience as recurrent stress, and intense pain decreases the levels of endorphin (a natural substance that relieves pain) inside the brain. This increases their vulnerability and must be offset through pain management. Time is critical with suicidal individual. They are in jeopardy and may be within hours or days of succumbing to their condition. Immediately impacting their pain is the only way to save their lives.

The toughest part for suicide grievers is not

having the answers. Losing someone you love or someone with whom you are very close through suicide is the most devastating loss of all. Equally disturbing is the fact that nothing in life can prepare one for the suicide of a loved one. Often, you are left with persistent questions of why. Let's take a look at some of the more common concerns.

1. <u>Why did this happen</u>? It happened because your loved one felt psychological pain so severe and unbearable that he or she believed it could only be stopped by death. The pain was caused by depression, which was caused by something in his or her life and/or brain. Those who have committed suicide probably did not do it <u>to</u> their loved ones; they did it <u>for</u> themselves. For some reason, life became too painful and unbearable for them. Consciously or unconsciously, they determined to stop their life on earth. The alternative of death seemed better than living in this physical realm.

   Jeff Perritte, a former student and young mentor, has developed the "Loss of Center Core" model as to why a person would take his or her own life. He states that one's removal from the "center core" of his or her life is the single greatest cause of suicide. In other words, losing one's "center core" meaning in life can be defined as the loss of what most closely defined one's existence. When this phenomenon is removed, then the suicidal person decides there is nothing worth living for now. The "danger signs" of suicide that a person demonstrates are the person's reaction to the ultimate loss.

2. Why didn't I know? Most people don't know the symptoms of depression or the warning signs of suicide. Many of those suffering depression hide it, and some suicidal individuals don't show any signs of their risk or danger. Even when there is some concern, it is very hard to accept that someone you know so well is in mortal danger of suicide. If your personal perspective is life affirming and non-suicidal, it's even more difficult to recognize the opposite states in others.

3. Why didn't my loved one tell me? Some may find it hard to ask for help or admit to mental illness, even if it may be temporary. Some

may feel shame at being suicidal. Intense pain is distracting and consuming. It makes those suffering extremely self-centered and takes away any sense of control. It doesn't mean that they didn't care for or love those suffering because of the loss. Tunnel vision is part of being suicidal.

4. <u>Why didn't somebody do something</u>? Even professionals sometimes have a hard time seeing that someone is suicidal. Misplaced concerns about privacy and confidentiality may deter warnings to others. There are no reliable predictors to suicide.

5. <u>Why do I feel like I'm going crazy</u>? You may have suffered the greatest and most horrible emotional shock of your life. Suicide is a severe traumatic loss that is usually sudden, unexpected, and violent. You feel betrayed, out of control, disoriented, and hurt. This is what happens after suicide. Nobody is ready for it, and it overwhelms anyone it directly affects.

6. <u>Why can't I get over this</u>? The loss is too

fresh, and you are traumatized. The first weeks and months are very hard, and your emotions may be in turmoil for a long time. You never really "get over" your loss, but you eventually come to terms by resolving to "learn to live with it."

7. <u>Why doesn't anything help me?</u> You can be helped. Start by seeing your doctor. He or she may be able to recommend services or medications that may help. You can go to a suicide loss support group or talk to a grief specialist, counselor, or clergy person. You can find information and people to talk to online who may also help you.

Perritte also presents an insight concerning the initial outpouring of sympathy regarding a suicide. Although well intentioned, we may actually indulge in overkill when attempting to express sympathy. Certainly, there is a heightened sense of responsibility to keep the survivors from harming themselves. However, there is an acute difference between what we may term a "sloppy agape" type of love and genuine sincerity that does not suffocate those in grief. Perritte calls for an authentic response as he profoundly proclaims in the following poem:

I Reject Your Sympathy

The pain is here and it's enough.
You are fake. I call your bluff.
Help you give, but not received.
A friend I thought, I once believed.
I question you; yes, I dare.
My pain is not what I cannot bear.

Added burdens are what you bring.
Another day longer 'till I can sing.
Until you're real, let me be.
I reject your sympathy.

On my phone and at my door.
The suffocation I cannot ignore.
Your contract with kindness, I release,
if your holy advice will finally cease.
One thing you waste and that is time,
playing your masked skit like a mime.

A friend I could use; yes, indeed.
Someone to replant my inner seed.
Until that person is here with me,

I will always reject your sympathy.

Clearly, his perceptive insights cause us to be aware that inappropriate sympathy is worse than none at all and may cause more emotional damage in the end.

Question:
When does grief become abnormal?

The definition of the words "normal" and "abnormal" depend upon individual perception. What one considers normal may, in fact, appear overtly abnormal to another. Therefore, a question arises as to when grief completes the metamorphosis from normal to abnormal. The following is presented to provide clues for identifying such various classifications of grief reactions.

Individuals who have not appropriately initiated, resolved or processed their grief may find themselves experiencing residual trauma and impaired functioning. When grief is used as a "scapegoat" for justifying unacceptable behaviors, then some degrees of abnormality may be occurring. Recall the variables regarding how a person grieves—personality temperament, belief system, value set and his or her relationship with the loss. It is common for degrees of grief to fluctuate from 12-18 plus months. Although we do not get over a loss, we do learn to live with it.

The following ideas may aid in the determination between what is considered normal grief and what appears to have become abnormal.[vi]

1. When the loss becomes a person's identity. The person feels he or she becomes "someone" by seeking attention due to grief. In other words, the person becomes the widow of the deceased rather than being his or her own person.

2. When a person cannot discuss any subject without his or her grief becoming the central content of the conversation.

3. When a person cannot speak of the deceased without reverting into an intense response as if the grief had freshly happened.

4. When a minor event or situation, such as seeing a funeral procession on the street,

brings out an intense grief reaction.

5. When radical changes in lifestyle occur soon after the loss. Examples include making hasty major decisions such as selling the house or suddenly abusing controlled substances such as alcohol or drugs.

6. When the grieving excludes family and friends from his or her individual processing of the grief.

7. When the grieving cannot deal with or distribute the possessions of the deceased.

8. When the grieving move into a long history of depression that results in guilt and/or self-rejection, then resulting in low self-esteem.

9. When the grieving has a definite denial or avoidance in grief-related rituals.

10. When the grieving turns to self-destructive behaviors in order to try to resolve his or her grief.

Question:

How can I find spiritual comfort during a time of grief?

My first experience in grief resulted in notice-able despair. Many attempted to resurrect my former fervor for life through texts that examined the issue of death, yet I was disillusioned with these standardized books. Thus, I rendered their efforts quite fruitless. In fact, I harbored such disdain for my grief-stricken state that upon one friend's impassioned plea to read selected scriptures from the Bible, I refrained and entertained anger with God instead.

If such a chilly disposition constitutes your feel-ings regarding the Bible and its contents, perhaps your grief has also reached dangerous limits. I was not willing to be open to God and let His Word change my perspective. When I was in the different stages of the grief process, I did not even try to employ God's Word in my personal itineraries. I was too busy feeling sorry for myself concerning my loss. As I continued in a deep sadness, I began to despair. I felt so weak and inadequate. Finally, I was desperate enough to read the Bible. When I became willing to be open to God's Word, I found out it really works!

You may ask yourself one important question at this juncture, "Am I willing *to be willing* to give God's Word a chance to change my heart and mind and give me comfort that I need so desperately now?" Regardless of your answer, I want to present a challenge. Start each day of your life with a brief prayer: "Heavenly Father, please make Yourself better known to me. Fill my life. Take charge of it and use it as You see fit." If you really mean that prayer, I believe some incredibly wonderful things will happen to you!

I discovered that the Bible reveals much about people who have had the same needs that I have! Perhaps by now you are thinking something like, "It sounds good, but I have heard such hype before." Perhaps your experience with the Bible continues to elicit the same empty experience. Let me assure you that I am aware of this problem. I suggest that you ask God to help you reject your feelings and by faith take Him at His word. Again, Mark 9:24 states it perfectly, "I believe; help my unbelief."

When I rejected my feelings and began to trust God by faith, reading the Bible changed my perspective. I soon took the stand on which I now rest my case—I avowedly accept the Bible as the authoritative Word of God that presents the standard of faith and practice. It is the revelation of God's action with His people throughout the ages.

The Bible contains a message of hope to the human race that could not have been the mere product of human minds. Truths are set forth in Scripture that human beings could never have known had they not been divinely revealed. The fulfillment of prophecy bears witness to the inspiration of the Bible, as does its message. It tells us the kind of God we have; it reveals the awful nature and consequence of sin; it points out the way of salvation and the real purpose of life. Thus, we must be conscious of making our daily activities and subsequent beliefs contingent upon it.

If you need spiritual comfort and renewal, please study the following scriptures:

Facing Grief
Romans 8: 26–29. Grief refines.
Philippians 1:21. To die is gain.
2 Corinthians 1:3–4. Comfort in grief.

Depression
Psalms 23. He restores my soul.

Hebrews 13:5. God will not leave you.
Jeremiah 29:11. Plans for your good.

Doubts
John 3:16. God loves.
Romans 10:9–10. Agree with God.

Fear
2 Timothy 1:7. God gives sound mind.

Strength
Isaiah 40:28–30. The Lord shall renew strength.
2 Corinthians 12:9. Grace is sufficient for you.

Peace
Romans 5:1–6. Peace with God.
Isaiah 26:3. Perfect peace.

Comfort
John 14:1–3. Let not your heart be troubled.
Philippians 1:6. Completion of faith.

Position
1 Thessalonians 4:13–18. Grieve not as those
who have no hope.
2 Corinthians 5:1–10. Absent from the body,

present with the Lord.

Read and believe Scripture. It tells about the goodness of God and the immortality of the soul. As you trust the Bible, you will find a deep resolve and conviction welling up in your mind that His words are true indeed!

CHAPTER NINE

Practical Preparation

Question:
What should I do when a death occurs?

Eventually, a relative or friend may turn to you in a time of bereavement. As a result, you may face new and sudden responsibilities that must be addressed rather quickly. It is important to remember that any crisis at this point creates an emergency for the family of the deceased. In such instances, their coping capabilities may rest largely upon your ability to execute expedient and appropriate action. Thus, it is wise to initiate contact with the following individuals so that necessary arrangements and decisions may be made with relative ease:

1. <u>Attending physician or medical examiner</u>. If a doctor was attending the deceased, he or she will help you start making arrangements. If the death was the result of violence or could have possibly been the result of a criminal act, the medical examiner must examine the circumstances. The police can also be quite helpful with certain, minute details only their authority may address.

2. <u>Funeral director</u>. Contact a funeral director you respect. He or she will advise you and guide your selections. You should feel no embarrassment discussing with the director your desires and ability to pay. The staff should be helpful in making suitable arrangements that are appropriate for the family per your specifications. The funeral director should also secure necessary burial permits and death certificates, provide counsel regarding actual funeral plans, place obituary and funeral notices in local newspapers,

and contact the media. Furthermore, if the deceased is to be taken to a distant point for burial, the funeral director should make the necessary arrangements for transit. Remember, the funeral director's job is to assist you in every way to make the funeral a memorial service that is an expression of your faith and life.

3. <u>The minister</u>. The minister will offer comfort to the family and make himself or herself available to all who need special counseling. He or she will also provide direction regarding the appropriate sequence of events within the actual funeral service. Make sure you designate the tone of the service. For instance, verbally note with the director prior to the event if you prefer to celebrate the life of the deceased as opposed to dwelling upon his or her absence. The minister will also collaborate closely with the funeral director in planning the details.

4. <u>Family and Friends</u>. You may need to call members of the family and close friends to inform them of the death that has occurred. You should ask others to aid you in making such necessary calls as well as meeting the needs of the many

experiencing painful grief. Keep in mind, most who are close to the situation will want to express through both word and deed that they care.

Question:

How can I get my business affairs in proper order?

Upon learning of the death of a loved one, various business and personal matters confront the family—all issues to address with swift resolve. In order to help families during this time of adjustment, many governmental agencies as well as banking facilities offer financial advising services that can save survivors time and unnecessary confusion. Family members may call upon such institutions and arrange an appointment with one of the advisors. Working with a member or members of the family, the advisor will prepare a comprehensive written checklist. The checklist will include defining the proper authorities to be notified and certain practical measures that should be taken. He or she will also note any documents or other basic information that will be required in filing claims for such benefits as Social Security,

Civil Service, Life Insurance, Pension Plans, Retirement Plans, Teacher's Benefits, and Veteran's Benefits.

Knowing the exact documents needed in filing various claims gives family members an opportunity to assemble required data and avoid repeated conferences with claims personnel at various governmental agencies.

Despite the resources of expertise indicated above, general advisement does not replace the need for legal and other professional services. In settling the business and personal affairs of the deceased, the services of attorneys, public accountants, etc., may be required in resolving legal matters, fulfilling accounting requirements, settling life insurance claims and filing sufficient reports with the Internal Revenue Service. **Under no circumstances should a general advisor attempt to provide these ancillary forms of counsel.**

Next, the following necessary actions may prove invaluable to those who wish to assist those in grief yet feel helpless as to how to proceed. Furthermore, because many deaths occur at night, the first ten items on the following list can be accomplished in deference to those details that must wait until later in the daytime hours.

Immediate Needs:

1. Notify the appropriate representative within the family's church.

2. Make necessary telephone calls immediately, especially those where travel time may be a factor.

3. Arrange for someone to spend the night with the family and give medication to those who have obtained a doctor's prescription.

4. Answer and keep a list of incoming telephone calls as well as any visitor arrivals and/or departures.

5. Assume responsibility for small children and arrange for them to be cared for outside the home for a day or two if the family so desires.

6. Check food supplies at the residence, and make a grocery list, keeping in mind that friends and neighbors will bring food as well.

7. Arrange for someone to keep a careful record of food, offers of assistance, and other details.

8. Note who may need assistance with clothing. Some washing and ironing may be necessary in preparation for the service, etc.

9. Select clothing to be worn by the deceased.

10. Help select the pallbearers and gather information that will be needed by the funeral director for the obituary.

Later Needs:

11. Locate all papers pertaining to the deceased, such as the will, insurance policies, and other documents. Do not throw away any papers until it has been determined that they are not needed.

12. Determine which relatives are to stay in the home. Some guestroom preparation may be necessary.

13. Schedule an appointment with the funeral

director. Deliver clothing to be worn by the deceased at that time.

14. Check the will for any special funeral instructions.

15. Notify employer and professional associates.

16. Arrange to have someone remain at the residence for security purposes during the funeral.

17. Request meeting times with the attorney and insurance agent.

Conclusion

T hroughout this text, you have been confronted with various questions and answers regarding loss and the subsequent grief process. You now have several options from which to choose. You may choose to dwell on your grief in a morbid way; you may choose to feel sorry for yourself; you may choose to make other people miserable; or you may choose to find a new normal life and help others because of your experience.

Although you would not have asked for the experience of grief, it has likely resulted in much truth about issues of both life and death. Above all, I hope you have learned that we do not know how to live until we know how to die!

Remember, the heart of this book is summarized

in the following steps. Thus, as stated earlier, when you get "sick and tired of being sick and tired," consider your next steps:

1. ADMIT IT!
    Boldly say aloud, "My loved one is dead because of_____ (fill in the blank)."

2. VENT IT!
    I encourage you to talk, cry, scream—just get your deep, emotional feelings out of your system.

3. RELEASE IT!
    Release your feelings. Then release your loved one. Give him or her permission to be deceased and present with God until you join your loved one again.

Finding a new normal life without the deceased is a deeply personal journey. Keep these helpful step stones of progress in mind as you bring some closure to your loss.

I continue to love you! There will always be a special love for that person.

Thank you! You are deeply appreciative of all his or her contributions to your life.

I forgive you. Choose to forgive any infraction that hurt you. As a result, it becomes easier to capitalize on the positive aspects of the relationship.

Goodbye. No one can ever take his or her place, yet new places may be created if you desire.

Direction and Comfort

This book has been written in general terms so that it could be understood by a wide range of individuals that have come or will come in contact with the process of grief. Each person who has read this book has probably identified with some dimension of death, dying, and grief. Each person has looked at the subject from a different pair of eyes or personal perspective.

My goal has been to help people reflect upon their individual feelings and attitudes related to losses and grief. Perhaps the reflective thinking has helped to open the door on a taboo subject, and the book will become an aid to helping people help themselves. It may also serve as the necessary compass or blueprint from which we may glean direction and comfort others.

More than three hundred years ago, a philosopher said, "The human mind is as little capable to contemplate death for any length of time as the eye is able to look at the sun." It is normal to advance and retreat in our viewing of the aspects of death. Yet, the need to face the subject remains as important as ever—if we are to be prepared for that time.

Furthermore, I have now disclosed how little I know about the mystery of death and grief. In many ways, I am ashamed of how limited my knowledge actually is. Yet, never have I enjoyed life more than when I started having the courage to begin facing death and living life.

Best-selling author, Eugenia Price, once stated, "One day all my question marks will be jerked into exclamation points!" A former student and young mentor, Lee Payne, (who is also a quadriplegic) has perhaps said it best, "The loss that I thought I could not live with has provided meaning and direction in my life that I can not live without!" Finally, I wish to reiterate the conclusion of the book of Ecclesiastes:

"Here is my final conclusion.
Trust God and keep His Commandments."

-Ecclesiastes 12:13-

Endnotes

[i] Ideas used by permission. Elizabeth Kubler-Ross, *On Death and Dying*, New York: Macmillan Publishing Company, 1969.

[ii] Tim LaHaye, *Spirit-Controlled Temperament*, Tyndale House Publishers, 1966.

[iii] Carolyn Roberts, Ph.D. is a licensed Marriage and Family Therapist in Los Angeles, California, and consultant to the Marilyn Hilton M.S. Achievement Center's program, Living Well: An Integrative Approach to Living with Multiple Sclerosis, a joint project between the U.C.L.A. Department of Neurology and the National Multiple Sclerosis Society.

[iv] Ideas adapted and used by permission. Larry Richards and Paul Johnson, *Death and the Caring Community* Portland, OR: Multnomah Press, 1980.

[v] For further resources and information on suicide grief, you may wish to refer to a website hosted by Tony Salvatore, http://lifegard.tripod.com.

[vi] Ideas adapted by permission from Richard James, *Crisis Intervention Strategies*, Brooks/Cole, 2001.

Printed in the United States
68836LVS00002B/463-483